The Art of Managing the Sizzle

INTERNATIONAL
Real World Training Solutions

www.pencominternational.com | 800.247.8514

©2004, 2010 by Pencom International

All rights reserved. No part of this book may be reproduced or transmitted in any form or by any means, electronic or mechanical, including photocopying, recording or by any informational storage or retrieval system — except by a reviewer who may quote brief passages in a review to be printed in a magazine or newspaper — without permission in writing from the publisher. For information contact Pencom International, 11776 West 53rd Place, Arvada, CO 80002, (303) 595-3991, (800) 247-8514.

Thank you.

ISBN: # 1-879239-44-2

PUB-515
12/2010

Written by TJ Schier for Pencom International
Edited by Bill Nelson and Kristen Kent
Cover and interior design by Deborah Henckel

CONTENTS

INTRODUCTION 3

Chapter 1 7
Now That's Service That Sells!

Chapter 2 15
Hospitality

Chapter 3 31
Do You Know Who I Am?

Chapter 4 43
Which Path Am I On?

Chapter 5 53
The Carryout Experience

Chapter 6 59
Situational-Selling

Chapter 7 67
The Manager (That's You!)

Chapter 8 79
The New Players

Chapter 9 95
Leading the Revolution

Chapter 10 105
Coaching on Game Day

Chapter 11 117
Reinforcing the Message

Chapter 12 127
Rallying the Troops

Chapter 13 139
Marketing

Chapter 14 149
Action Plan

Appendix A 157
Appendix B 163
Appendix C 165
Appendix D 166
Appendix E 168

Now That's **SERVICE THAT SELLS!**

To Chris, Chris, Jeff and George — the trailblazers of hospitality!

introduction

INTRODUCTION

Most restaurant guests have had service experiences go terribly wrong. And the funny thing is, many employees — and even managers — at the time would say they had done a good job, or at least what their company would've wanted them to. How would they know? They're simply a product of the environment the company and managers have created.

The typical full-service restaurant breaks down its "steps of service" this way:

- Greet
- Seat
- Take order
- Food delivery
- Check back
- Suggest dessert
- Thank

These steps provide guidance but allow for little flexibility and personality. After all, shouldn't it be the guests who determine what kind of service they want?

Airlines, for instance, still review how to fasten a seatbelt prior to takeoff. Is there any flier left on the planet who doesn't know how to buckle up? As a very frequent-flier myself, do I like being drawn through the whole evacuation process? I know there are 50 ways to leave your lover but only four ways to get off the airplane. Come on, adapt with the times and update outdated service steps.

Your guests today need more than "G.E.D. Service" — Greet, Eat, Delete. When I talk to servers, managers and hosts in the habit of delivering uninspired service, they honestly think they're doing what's expected of them.

What's their frame of reference? The experiences they receive when dining out. Most haven't been to a fine-dining establishment or stayed at a five-star hotel to understand the breadth of the gap. They can't deliver great service — *Service That Sells!* — because they have no idea what it looks and sounds like.

> **Employees are simply a product of the environment the company and managers have created.**

introduction

> If yours is a restaurant churning people through a cookie-cutter experience, you can't expect to survive ...

If yours is a restaurant churning people through a cookie-cutter experience, you can't expect to survive, let alone thrive. Guests are more savvy and thus more demanding than ever before. It's either their way or no way.

Forget being 1% better at 100 things — it's time to step out. Be unique, be great and be different. Period. Crush the competition by providing *the* service experience that can't be found anywhere else. Own your guests by creating loyalty.

Over the past few years, airlines, hotels, websites and other businesses have been customizing services according to guests' needs. Sign up for a frequent-stay program at a leading hotel chain and you can enter personal choices for a welcome beverage and snack, not to mention the type of pillow you want upon arrival. Gone are the good ol' days of "smoking or non?" Go online and retail sites make recommendations based on what type of items have been viewed.

People are asking for what they want, when they want it and how they want it. Early on, who would have thought carryout business would make up as much as 20% of many full-service restaurants' sales mix? Not offering to-go? Many guests will just drive down the road to those who do. Heck, you may have to deliver it curbside just to compete.

The skeptic in you may be saying: "My guests don't expect fine-dining service. Why should I focus on it?" Deliver the unexpected! It doesn't matter if your restaurant is quick-service, family dining or casual theme, you can set yourself apart by delivering the unexpected and out of the ordinary — exactly what guests want!

Ideas are just the beginning — it's how you execute them that makes all the difference in the world. *Now That's Service That Sells!* will show you how to succeed. Here we go.

5

chapter one

©2010 pencom international · www.pencominternational.com

CHAPTER 1

Now *That's* Service That Sells!

> You can't stop when you're satisfied, only when the guest is delighted and loyal.

For more than a dozen years and counting, **the best-selling book *Service That Sells!*** (Pencom International Press) transformed the service guests receive and helped countless restaurants build sales through improved suggestive-selling techniques. So why mess with success? Why write a sequel?

Think of this book not as a sequel, but another chapter in an evolving industry. The marketplace has changed dramatically. Fast-casual concepts, for instance, have given rise to a hybrid experience between quick-serve and full-serve, creating a new line of competitors and diminishing available sales dollars.

With the explosion of fast casual, guests have increased control of their dining experience and demand "serve-us service." Great food at lower prices combined with the ability to control the time of experience is changing the way restaurants do business. The new mantra is: "Treat me the way *I* want to be treated, not the way you want to treat me." It's now pronounced *serve-us*, not service.

In some industries, choices are limited.

If you need to book a flight, there are few airlines to choose from, depending on the market, and usually few price differences. Loyalty is easy to earn. Almost by default you have to frequent one brand.

> The new mantra is: "Treat me the way *I* want to be treated, not the way you want to treat me."

With hotels and restaurants, however, there is a wide range of options and prices. Loyalty is tougher to earn. For some consumers, your products may not be right, so your restaurant isn't even considered. For other consumers, yours may be just one of countless possibilities. How do you stand out from the crowd?

chapter one

A shipping company's ad sums up the guest focus today: "The most important package is yours." In a restaurant environment, guests don't care how much your staff knows, how good your training program is or how many meals you serve. They care about one thing — their experience. They want it their way on their terms and they're not afraid to tell everyone if it's not right. In fact, there are plenty of websites where guests can post comments for all to read about the unsatisfactory experiences they had.

As guests and competitors raise the bar, it has become necessary to evolve with the times or fade away. *Now That's* Service That Sells! focuses on what you can do to create high-frequency guests — those who are the most loyal. Numerous books have been written about the link between guest loyalty and long-term profitability. But understanding the link and doing something about it are two different things.

Until the late 1980s, competition was minimal and any form of service brought in business. Competition and restaurant growth exploded in the '90s. Restaurants that simply provided service were left behind. *Service That Sells!* became the norm as Pencom International promoted its message across the country and even the world.

Guests, meanwhile, continued to become more selective and demanding. Satisfaction does not equal happiness. Satisfaction does not drive sales. Shooting for "satisfied" will spell demise. To thrive, restaurants have to aim higher. It's time to step up how you deliver service so you can say: *"Now That's* Service That Sells!"

Put simply, *Service That Sells!* is delivering hospitality and a customized experience for each guest the way he or she wants it to be. The formula is easy — execution each and every day is not.

Service Mechanics. They're the tasks of filling the needs of guests. Many companies call these "steps of service." If the steps are without personality, chances are they could be replaced with a bit of technology (place your own order, for instance) or easily surpassed by your competitor.

Hospitality. Not only is it what you say, it's how you say it. Hospitality screams: "We care!" It drives loyalty and frequency. It builds sales by eliminating the competition from guests' minds. It's the emotional attachment you make with guests.

Customized Experiences. Why are guests visiting? Celebration? Date? In a hurry? Relaxing? Family night out? First time? Regular? They all have different sets of needs and cannot all be treated with the same service steps. Deliver what guests want, not what the company wants.

If you execute effectively in these three areas, sales will increase. It won't happen, however, by itself. Success is in the hands of the manager and staff. So, to ensure you can say *Now That's Service That Sells!*, managers need to:

> Manage the sizzle. True change starts at the top. Many will read this book, but how many will put it into action? Will you? What's important is talked about constantly. What's important gets resources — time, effort and energy to ensure it happens.

> Motivate the staff. If the desire is to improve the guest experience, enhance the employee experience. If employees don't feel taken care of, they won't take care of guests. Once knowledge has been imparted, the key is to get the staff to put it into action for the benefit of guests as well as sales and profits.

Not every idea presented will work in every restaurant. Pick the ones with the greatest chance of success. Use them to enhance strengths and leverage competitive advantages to add distinction to guests' experiences. Make the competition suffer!

I use the term "guests" versus "customers." Customers shop in retail — they may or may not buy something. Guests have already made the decision to purchase something the minute they pull into the parking lot of your restaurant. Therefore, you need to treat them differently than someone deciding if they'll purchase something.

Today's guests are savvy, demanding, value-conscious and not prone to loyalty. If so many people aren't even loyal to their spouses or companies, how are they going to be loyal to a restaurant?

chapter one

You've probably seen those pictures called "photomosaics." From a distance, they appear to be just another picture. Up close, however, you can see hundreds of little photos. The uniqueness is the detail. Otherwise, it's just another picture. In a restaurant, the interaction points between the guests and your staff are the difference-makers. Delivering *Service That Sells!* is all about "sizzle points" — the details in the dining picture — that wow guests and create a unique visit to your restaurant. Consider:

> While boarding a shuttle at a rental-car business on a hot Raleigh day, a cooler filled with ice-cold bottled waters helped provide a wow on a routine ride back to the airport.

Now *That's* Service That Sells!

> A ho-hum wake-up call becomes a wow:
>
> Guest: "I need a wake-up call at 5 a.m. tomorrow morning."
>
> Front Desk: "That's early! Can I put another one in for 5:15 a.m. just to be sure you get up?" Guest: "Certainly!"

Now *That's* Service That Sells!

> A quick-serve restaurant doesn't have an order ready when the guest pulls up to the drive-thru window. The driver is asked to park (*aagh!*). A minute or so later a crew member comes up, apologizes for the inconvenience and informs the guest that the drink and fry have been upsized at no charge.

Now *That's* Service That Sells!

A restaurant experience is a series of interactions which, by themselves, don't add up to anything memorable. By providing unique experiences at each point, a picture emerges — a very different one than your competition provides. Sounds easy and it would be if all guests' needs were the same. All guests are not created equal nor are their expectations. Restaurants can't treat everyone the same way — OK — and expect to improve guest frequency.

As far as frequency goes, guests fall into **three** categories:

Regulars.

1 They are high-frequency users who go out of their way to eat at your restaurant. Bonded to the brand, they're known by all and won't ever be lost unless taken for granted.

Rotators.

2 They enjoy your brand but because of inconsistent experiences they don't frequent you as much as they should or want to. You tend to lose one and gain one, never seeming to get ahead. This group has the potential to be high frequency. Find out what their needs are and take care of them.

Ghosts.

3 They don't like your brand. Whether it's the type of food, location or a past bad experience, this group will never visit. Time to forget them.

Bill Cosby once said: "I don't know the key to success, but the key to failure is trying to please everyone." In applying *Service That Sells!* techniques, focus on your regulars and rotators, showering them with out-of-the-ordinary hospitality and addressing their individual needs so they can and will dine at your restaurant more often.

chapter one

Guest frequency stems from building loyalty to a brand — not only in terms of menu, atmosphere and service, but also the employees who put a face on what you're offering. Over time, however, many companies struggle to deliver the basics. Fixated on growing the number of units or hitting earnings per share, they make decisions at the expense of employees and guests to drive short-term gains. Systems and other constraints prohibit even basic delivery of service. The end result? Guests aren't loyal if they're treated like a number or transaction.

"Good enough" is the enemy of greatness. "Satisfied" is a far cry from "delighted" or "loyal." Slight improvements in frequency and service levels produce huge gains in sales and profits. It's a phenomenon similar to professional golf. Tiger Woods led the 2002 PGA Tour in money (over $6.9 million) and stroke average (69.0). Drop down the list one shot to the person who averaged 70 per round and he made only $1.3 million. One shot per day! What can managers do to get one more guest in per day?

With the explosive growth in the number of restaurants and choices, service in many cases has degraded into a series of average experiences. In many towns, guests can eat out every night at a different restaurant for a month (or more) and never eat at the same place twice. With competitors struggling to get food to the table, there is a tremendous opportunity to set your restaurant apart.

> **Ask yourself: What bothers and frustrates guests?** What will they be letting you know about? Why don't they return?

They're treated like a number
("Four for dinner?" "Here's your pager — wait in the bar.")

 They're served by insincere employees who don't seem to care or are inadequately trained to handle the business.

They're ignored or "processed" through the meal.

 They're met by managers who don't want to hear feedback or are unresponsive when it's given.

©2010 pencom international · www.pencominternational.com

Guest service is tough. Why?

Each guest is different.
Their needs change depending on why they're visiting.

So, how does your restaurant take care of an ever-changing set of needs? The first step is to figure out who the guests are and why they're visiting. When asked for the definition of pornography, a judge once replied: "I may not be able to define "pornography," but I know it when I see it."

Outstanding service is the same way — you know it when you see it or experience it. Without it, it's just another visit.

chapter two

CHAPTER 2

Hospitality

> I can't describe it, but I know it when I see it.

Managers who focus on sales, profits and managing service will struggle to prosper in the long term. It's too easy to be replicated. Competitors will just come along and mimic the tangible — the menu and the prices. Shoot, they may even lower the prices.

It's difficult, on the other hand, to copy the *intangible* — the hospitality your staff delivers on a daily basis. Hospitality drives sales and profits, not the other way around. It's the difference maker, the catapult to greater heights.

The words *service* and *hospitality* tend to be used interchangeably, but they're very different. Service involves steps and tasks to fill a need. A vending machine dispensing a soda is service. Delivering food is service. Hospitality is the desire to serve others. It's the flair and personalization of going through the service steps in a unique manner. It's the sizzle that makes you say: "Wow, that place gets it!"

> **The words *service* and *hospitality* tend to be used interchangeably, but they're very different.**

At every contact point guests have with staff, facility and product, they form opinions that sizzle, fizzle or come off neutral. Delivering *Service That Sells!* hospitality ensures those impressions *sizzle*. Without it, your restaurant will become just another choice in the marketplace (or one to avoid).

The problem is, **employees and managers often don't know what hospitality looks or sounds like.** It's three-dimensional, not merely words in a book. Tone, body language and actual spoken words determine if it is indeed hospitality or another robotic server reciting canned sayings mandated by management. Hospitality is a choice, a state of mind. It's not a program to be implemented and quickly forgotten — it's who you are.

chapter two

The ideas presented in these pages must be practiced with your staff. Reading words and repeating them to guests without flair, passion or sincerity is actually worse than saying nothing at all. Guests can smell a phony a mile away.

The best way to master the art of delivering hospitality is to experience it firsthand. There are two alternatives: send employees to observe restaurants skilled at hospitality or use your own hospitable environment as a teaching tool.

If you send employees elsewhere, it's critical to review the visit and relate the experience to their own workplace situation. If you opt for an in-house approach, set up a series of role-plays during which employees can begin to understand the difference between service and hospitality. For example, greeting and escorting guests the proper way instead of chirping: "Two?" (See Appendix A for other role-play examples).

Guests form opinions within seconds — seconds waiting to be acknowledged, to be sat, to place a drink order, to get and pay the check. Eye contact and a warm smile go a long way in helping guests form a positive impression. These simple behaviors also minimize dead time and underscore your restaurant's hospitality focus.

Typically, employees today don't have a hospitality skill set when they arrive. They've grown up watching TV personalities and athletes talking smack, being rude, using slang and dressing differently. It's up to managers to teach the right way of doing things.

With the understanding that restaurant concepts have different types of guests and levels of expectations, here are a few words of advice to enlighten the staff:

Avoid terms such as:

* "Dudes," "man" or "guys." ("Hey, guys!" when it's a family entering).
* "Cool," "awesome," "kickin," "wicked."
* "Whatever," "OK," "No problem (when used instead of "You're welcome")."
* "No" or "Can't." Teach employees to offer alternatives: "What we can offer is…" Or: "What I can do for you is…" Or: "Yes, for a slight charge."
* "It's our policy." Yeah, and it's the guest's policy not to return when treated in this manner.

©2010 pencom international · www.pencominternational.com

To help your staff move from service to hospitality, role play various interactions position by position. Consider using a camcorder or "spy-cam" shooting from the point of view of the role-playing guests. This will allow servers or hosts to see what they look like through the eyes of those they're serving.

When this is done, typical employee responses heard are: "I didn't know I sounded like that." "Wow! Look how I'm holding my arms, I look mad." "Do I really sound like that?" "The second way sounds much more friendly." And so on. If a picture is worth 1,000 words, video is worth 10,000.

Let's go to the video.

▶ HOST

The host often provides the first and last impression guests have of a restaurant. And those impressions stick, especially if they're unique — positively or negatively. Too frequently, guests are greeted with bland, insincere welcomes.

Step one is the greeting, but how differently can it sound? Be specific with employees or this is what your guests will hear:

Typical Greetings

- "Two for dinner?"
- "Four for lunch?"
- "Dine-in or carryout?"
- "Smoking or non?"
- "One? Wanna sit in the bar?"
- "Just one?"
- "Name?"
- "The wait is about 20 minutes."
- "Need any high chairs or boosters?"

chapter two

Service That Sells! Greetings

- "Welcome! How is everyone today?"
- "Presents — what are we celebrating?"
- "You're in luck. The wait is only a short five to 10 minutes."
- "Will there be anyone else joining you tonight or are we going to take care of the two of you?"
- "Feel free to wait in our bar. We have an outstanding special on large draft beers!"
- Family or kids approach: "Here are some crayons and coloring pages to use while you wait."
- Guests' names are written on the guest check so the experience can be personalized.
- Names of guests are spelled like they sound in case another host or manager has to page them.

Now That's Service That Sells!

Typical Body Language

- Frowns, twirling hair, chatting with other hosts.
- Leaning on host stand.
- Arms crossed.
- Waiting for guests to initiate conversation or eye contact.
- Mechanical, robotic and/or standoffish.
- Sloppy, unprofessional appearance.

Service That Sells! Body Language

- Smiles.
- Willingness to approach guests and open doors.
- Quick to initiate conversation.
- Eye contact with every guest.
- Glad guest are visiting.
- Professional and polished appearance.

Now That's Service That Sells!

©2010 pencom international · www.pencominternational.com

After the initial greeting, hosts and/or seaters are responsible for seating guests. It can be done in a mechanical, scripted fashion or with flair and sizzle. Nothing like expecting the worst after an unenthusiastic greet and seat.

Typical Host Seating

- The Lurch Approach: "Follow me."
- Speedy, way out in front of guests.
- No conversation.
- Menus thrown onto the table.
- No menu knowledge or confidence to suggest items.

Service That Sells! Seating

- Guests are welcomed by name whenever possible.
- If guests are not recognized, they're asked if they've dined here before.
- First-time guests are shown the location of restrooms, stairs, items of interest, etc.
- Conversation is made with the nearest guest.
- Guests receive opened menus upon seating.
- Specials are pointed out along with confident suggestions: "My favorite entrée is the _____ and we're also featuring bottled beers for only $2. Please enjoy your dinner tonight!"

Now That's Service That Sells!

chapter two

In many cases, the host answers the phone and takes carryout orders. While not a step in the service sequence, the phone is a "pre-step." If it's not handled properly, why would potential guests want to try out the restaurant?

Typical Phone Answering

- Canned "Thanks for calling."
- So quick, guests can't understand a word.
- Immediate put on "ignore" (the next level of hold).
- Hard to hear because of loud background noise.
- Treated as an interruption of business.
- Lacking knowledge about directions, hours of operation and answers to FAQs.

Service That Sells! Phone Answering

- Upbeat with a unique greeting: "Thanks for calling _____, home of the _____. How may I help you?" Or: "Thanks for calling _____. We're featuring _____ tonight. How may I help you?"
- Hold time is minimized.
- The call is a priority with the realization that there is potential or immediate business on the other end of the line.
- Able to answer questions about directions from major intersections, hours of operations, menu, local attractions and other FAQs.

Now That's **Service That Sells!**

Hosts are also responsible for the final step of service: "Thank and invite back." The last impression of guests needs to be a positive one. Imagine taking a flight and the airline loses your luggage. Do you remember the free upgrade or the attentive flight attendant? Or is all forgotten once your luggage is nowhere to be found? Many hosts go through the motions, but are they delivering hospitality?

Typical Thanks

- No eye contact.
- Insincere.
- "Hope to see you again soon." (Is this really an invitation back? Sounds like, "Hope we didn't screw up so bad that you won't consider returning.")
- "Hey, thanks man for coming in." (Or other slang.)

Service That Sells! Thanks

- Door opened for departing guests.
- "Thanks again for choosing us to celebrate your birthday (or other special occasion). See you again soon!"
- "Was everything outstanding? Great! See you next week!"
- "It was our pleasure taking care of you today. Don't forget, we offer great fish specials on Fridays!"

Now That's Service That Sells!

Hosts play an important role in guests' experiences, yet how long do they get trained? And are they trained on:

- The menu.
- Answering the phone.
- Interacting with guests to make them feel welcome.
- The importance of their role.

Or are they trained in a cursory manner? "Here are the menus, these are the table numbers, seat the guests." Why let someone be a host and handle all the tables in the restaurant when he or she is trained far less than a server who has to take care of four or five tables?

To enhance the training of your hosts, have them shadow a server for a few hours. Walking a mile in a server's shoes will shed light on the impact that host actions have on service levels. For instance, how double-seating can cause service to slide. Hosts can also see the benefit of taking the drink order for a table when double-seating is unavoidable.

▶ SERVERS
Servers spend more time with guests than any other employee.
They handle most of the steps of service, interacting with each table as many as 15 times — or more. They make or break the experience.

Given the explosive growth of chain restaurants, it seems nearly anyone can be (or has been) a server. Yet not just anyone can create a wow at each and every guest contact point. It's critical to ensure your servers are the best of the best and show it every day. After all, they have one of the few jobs in which they determine and control their own income. Need to convince servers that hospitality is what they need to provide? Show them how much more money they'll be making!

Servers typically interact with guests when they: deliver the initial greeting, take the beverage order, deliver beverages, take the food order, deliver food, execute beverage refills, conduct checkbacks, complete table-maintenance chores, take dessert orders, deliver desserts, tender payment and offer thanks.

Of course, **they're doing all of this for multiple tables at one time, juggling multiple tasks.** These interactions start as they approach the table:

Typical Server Initial Contact

- "Any questions?"
- "Have you decided yet?"
- "Ready to order?"
- "Can I get anyone a super-sized, deluxe frozen margarita?" (Or other canned sales lines.)
- "Hey, guys! What's up?"
- "Hi, I'm _____ and I'll be your server today."

Can guests contain their excitement? What ever happened to "hello" and "welcome?"

Service That Sells! Initial Contact

- "Welcome to _____! How is everyone tonight?" Then one of the following:
- "Everyone ready for an outstanding meal?"
- "I understand it's your first time here. May I make a few suggestions?"
- "I see we've started off with some popular low-carb beers. Can I get everyone another?"
- "Presents — what are we celebrating?"
- "Welcome back. Great to see you again!"
- "You look like you're in a hurry. I'll get you in and out of here in no time."
- "It appears you'd like a little privacy. Just let me know if you need anything."
- "What's the special occasion for the group tonight? Are we going to need separate checks?"

chapter two

Be different. Be excellent. Make it special and unique. The key to delivering hospitality is to read the cues. Deliver the experience guests want, not what you want. During the course of the meal, servers will take numerous orders from guests — appetizers, drinks, entrées, desserts and after-dinner drinks. While Chapter 6 discusses situational selling in more detail, servers also have numerous sizzle points with each step of the meal.

Typical Order-Taking Responses

- "OK"
- Say nothing, just write it down.
- "No problem."
- "You can't make substitutions."
- "I'm not sure what the soup is today."
- "I don't know if it's good. I've never tried it."
- "I don't think it's that good."
- "Nobody's complained, so it must be OK."
- "Is that it?"
- "Anything else?"

Service That Sells! Order-Taking Responses

- "Great choice!"
- "It's one of our most popular dishes."
- "Great selection! That beer is our best seller!"
- "We get a lot of compliments on that."
- "Excellent."
- "It goes great with _____."
- "If you're in a hurry, you may want to order _____ instead of the well-done steak."
- "Would you like me to have the kids' meals out earlier?"
- "My pleasure. ..."
- "I'd be happy to. ..."

Now That's **Service That Sells!**

©2010 pencom international · www.pencominternational.com

A few other tips:

- Always let guests know what will happen next. For example, "Enjoy your drinks! I'll be back shortly with your appetizers."
- When delivering food items, describe the dish and don't reach in front of guests. Use the opposite hand. In other words, if they're on your right, serve with your left and vice versa (keep your elbow out of their face).
- Before leaving the table, ensure guests have everything they need (specific utensils, condiments, extra napkins, etc).

Typical Food Delivery

- "Who had the _____?"
- Plates are dropped on the table without a word.
- "Anything else?"
- Table is left crowded with glasses and previous plates.

Service That Sells! Food Delivery

- Unneeded plates and glasses are cleared prior to food delivery (and throughout the meal).
- All necessary utensils and condiments (steak sauce, for instance) are delivered ahead of time to prevent food from getting cold while the server gets those items.
- The meat (or main item) of the dish is placed closest to the guest if applicable.
- "Here's your hot, delicious _____."
- Women are served first if that appears to be the expectation of the table.
- Guests are asked to cut into a fish or steak order to make sure it's cooked to their liking. (No need to do so on chicken or pork.)

Now That's Service That Sells!

chapter two

As guests begin to eat, the next step is the checkback. As with earlier steps, there are several ways to proceed — with or without hospitality.

Typical Checkbacks

- "How is everything?"
- "Everything taste OK?" *(Do restaurants strive for "OK" or "All right?")*
- "Is it all right?"
- "Still working on that?"

Service That Sells! Checkbacks

- "Is your steak as good as I promised?"
- "Isn't the _____ outstanding?"
- "That beer sure is refreshing, isn't it?"
- "Was I right? Isn't the _____ excellent?"
- "May I remove _____ ?"
- "Still enjoying the _____ or may I remove it?"

Now That's **Service That Sells!**

The last step is the check presentation and tendering payment. Typically it's the last time servers will interact with guests. And, if guests don't get thanked by a host, it may be the last impression they have about the restaurant. Make it sizzle!

Typical Payment and Thanks

- "I'll be your cashier when you're ready."
- "I'm not trying to rush you, but I'll leave the check right here."
- "Separate checks? Why didn't you tell me at the beginning?"
- "Do you need change?"
- Counting change back at the table.
- "Are you done with my pen?"
- "Hope to see you again."

Service That Sells! Payment and Thanks

- "Thanks again for coming in. I'd be happy to take care of you on your next visit."
- "Congratulations again! See you next week!"
- "Enjoy the movie!"
- "I'll be right back with your change."
- "Thanks again for the opportunity to take care of you. Don't forget to try the _____ next time!"

Now That's Service That Sells!

Depending on the type of restaurant, the service assistants (buser sounds so limiting) and bartenders may interact with all or some guests at various points. Bartender interactions are similar to servers', but typically involve dialogue about drinks instead of food. There is a great opportunity in many restaurants, however, to enhance service with employees who assist servers.

Too many restaurants have their "busers" simply clean tables. Guests ask them for things and get "not my job" or "I'll get your server." Bad answers! Elevate busers to service assistants. After all, they provide assistance: filling water glasses, refilling drinks, running food, clearing plates and tables. Are they trained to interact with guests or do they simply complete tasks without ever saying a word?

Typical Buser

- Fills water, says nothing.
- Refills water and tea, says nothing.
- Guest: "Can I get another drink?" Buser: "I'll send over the server."
- Removes plates, says nothing. Or, if words are spoken, it's commonly, "Done with that?"
- "Can I have your plate?"
- Approaches table to clear it as guests depart, says nothing.

Service That Sells! Service Assistant

Now That's Service That Sells!

Starting to get it? Appendix B contains a handout (also available as a downloadable file at www.pencominternational.com) to use when training your staff on hospitality and the importance of how to say certain things. What a difference a few simple words, a smile and a positive, upbeat tone can make.

Now that you know how to treat every guest, let's dive into the specific needs of the different types of guests who visit so you can customize their experiences. It's your secret weapon, but it takes effort and practice to move from "typical" to *Service That Sells!*

chapter three

CHAPTER 3

Do you know who I am?

> "Cut my pizza into six slices,
> I don't think I can eat eight."
> — Yogi Berra

Ask employees: "What do we do?" Most responses will be along the lines of: "Serve food." How should they respond? "We pamper guests and create an enjoyable dining experience."

Harley Davidson doesn't sell motorcycles; it sells the Harley experience — allowing people to become an alter-ego. Disney isn't an amusement park, it's an experience. Great shows immerse you and make you feel like part of the action. Is your restaurant an *experience* or just a provider of food and service?

Opportunities abound to make your restaurant sizzle.
You do the math:

How many guests does your restaurant serve annually?

\+

How many times do guests interact with a person, product or facility during a typical visit?

=

Number of times ("sizzle points") guests decide if yours is *"a place"* or *"the place."*

chapter three

Everyone's volume and frequency is different, but a typical full-service restaurant sees more than 200,000 guests per year. On average, guests will interact with a host, bartender, server, service assistant, facility (restrooms, landscape, etc.) and product more than 25 times during the course of a visit. **That's more than 5 million opportunities to sizzle or fizzle each year!**

 What are the sizzle points in a restaurant? Appendix C contains a handout to raise awareness in this area with your staff. A typical guest interacts with the staff at the following points:

HOST
- Initial greeting and welcome.
- Taking names (if using names on guest checks or on a wait).
- Paging guests (if on a wait).
- Seating and escorting guests to the table.
- Thanking guests and inviting them back.

SERVER
- Initial greeting.
- Drink order, appetizer suggestion.
- Drink delivery, food order.
- Appetizer checkback, drink refills or reorders.
- Food delivery (multiple points including soup, salad, entrée, etc.).
- Food checkback, drink refills or reorders.
- Table maintenance.
- Dessert, after-dinner drink suggestions.
- Dessert and/or drink delivery.
- Check presentation.
- Tender payment.
- Thank guests and invite back as they depart.

OTHER EMPLOYEES (bartenders, service assistants, food runners)

Note: Depending on how the restaurant is staffed (no food runners, for instance), these things may be done by the server or host:

- Bar service while on a wait.
- Falling water glasses initial contact.
- Drink refills.
- Food delivery.
- Table maintenance.
- Clear and re-set table.
- Phone answering.
- Carryout process (order placement, suggestions, pick up).

FACILITY
- Front entry, doors, parking lot, landscape.
- Lobby, waiting area.
- Floors.
- Restrooms.
- Music, temperature levels.
- Tables, chairs.

PRODUCT
- Beverages.
- Appetizers.
- Salads/Soups.
- Entrées and sides.
- Desserts.
- After-dinner drinks.

chapter three

Does each point sizzle in your operation? Try this exercise with your employees: Have them try to draw their watch. Most look at it numerous times throughout the day, but chances are they can't even remember any details about it. Guests can be the same way — seen but not really known. They're invisible, treated as a series of steps, another four-top needing the check.

> **What does the perfect experience look like? It depends. Everyone's needs are different.**

Restaurants try to provide the same steps of service to everyone. Think about the last few occasions visiting a restaurant or bar. One time may have been a quick lunch, another you were working on a business deal and needed a little privacy. After work one night you met for drinks with friends. A dinner or two may have included family time with the kids or a quiet date with a spouse. Where did you go on all those visits? A favorite restaurant, the local lunch spot, the new place that opened in the neighborhood? It's a safe bet your needs were slightly different in each place and on each occasion. What does the perfect experience look like? It depends. Everyone's needs are different.

Ask employees and managers why guests are eating in the restaurant. You'll probably hear:

- Great food.
- Good service.
- Atmosphere.
- Friendly employees.
- Location.
- Price.
- Value.
- Unique décor.
- And so on.

Those reasons may help decipher why guests choose one restaurant over another, but they don't tell the whole story. Warning! If guests visit because the restaurant is close to their house or office, a competitor will build one closer. If they visit because of low prices, a competitor will lower its prices and a winless discounting war will erupt.

Now That's SERVICE THAT SELLS!

To truly understand what *Service That Sells!* is all about, you have to drill deeper. Why did guests decide to eat out or order carryout in the first place? The list of reasons forms the foundation for delivering *Service That Sells!*

- Heard about the restaurant and wanted to try it.
- No time to cook dinner.
- On the way to a ballgame, kid's event, practice, movie, and need a quick meal.
- Celebrating report cards, doctor visits, lost a tooth, personal success, milestone.
- Want a quiet night out.
- Conducting a business meeting.
- Have 45 minutes to eat lunch.
- The kids like the place.
- We like the place and the kids don't mind it.
- Have a group coming over and don't want to cook (carryout).
- Watching the game on TV (carryout)

To deliver *Service That Sells!*, it's important to discover **what guests need and want.** Asking questions provides this information. Think about salespeople. They ask questions to find out what clients are looking for, then make suggestions to enhance the purchase. A good salesperson would never call on a client without doing research first.

It's a little more difficult in restaurants. In most cases, you don't know who or how many are coming, or what the specific needs are. The staff must be able to determine those needs on the spot to provide the best experience possible.

Don't get caught up in making generalizations about guests. If someone has dined with you before, there's no need to give him or her the full tour and history of the restaurant just because it's a "step." If you get counted off for not providing drink refills quickly enough during a mystery shop, don't automatically bring refills to everyone. Not only will it cost you money, guests may not want them.

chapter three

Now, you may know all of this information, but are your guests receiving this customized level of service? If not, it's high time to train your employees to identify and meet guests' individual needs.

The great Yogi Berra also said: **"When you get to the fork in the road, pick it up."** Generally, there are two "forks" during a typical restaurant visit: Have they been there before? And are they in a hurry? Simply determining familiarity withthe restaurant and desired ace of the meal will enhance the service provided and put your staff on the way to delivering *Service That Sells!*

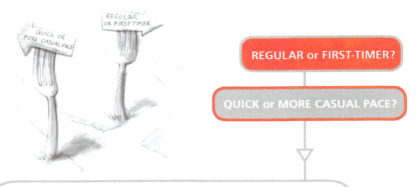

REGULAR or FIRST-TIMER?

QUICK or MORE CASUAL PACE?

HAVEN'T I SEEN YOU IN HERE BEFORE?

YES	NO
Thank guests for returning. Inform them of specials or features.	Welcome guests. Provide menu guidance and restaurant overview.

IN A HURRY?

YES	NO
Quicken the pace, taking the whole order at once (if desired), suggesting dessert earlier and dropping (and processing) the check quickly.	Deliver "silent service," addressing needs, letting guests enjoy the meal, not rushing the experience.

After your staff masters these two steps, move on to determining other needs discussed in the next chapter. Don't overwhelm employees. It's impossible to fix everything in a shift or a day.

In football, you get 10 yards in four plays or fewer and you get to keep going. Think how boring the game would be if teams had only four plays to go the length of the field. It wouldn't be very high scoring or exciting.

Same holds true for a restaurant. Set intermediate goals (first downs). Once the staff meets them, hand out rewards and update the goals. Kids try to complete mazes by starting at the beginning. It leads to dead ends, retracing steps and mistakes. After a few times, however, they start at the end and work backward. When looking to move to a higher level of service, take a similar approach. Don't start where service is today and work toward the goa with minor incremental changes. **Be bold! Start at the perfect experience and work back to today.**

So what do your different types of guests need?

chapter three

REGULARS

They're your bread and butter. You know who they are. Do your servers, hosts or cashiers?

Regulars want recognition. Think about the airlines. They treat their most frequent fliers to the most perks — do you? Regulars know how it's supposed to be. They're forgiving but demand consistency. Keep them loyal and don't ever take them for granted.

How Can You Sizzle?

Recognize your regulars. Welcome them and thank them for returning. Some restaurants have walls of fame with celebrity photos, but are they really the most valuable guests? Old Spaghetti Factory has a plaque in one of its restaurants honoring a guest who has dined there more than 4,000 times ... and counting! Regulars typically have a favorite table, chair or barstool — honor them! Eric Clapton started the memorabilia rage at Hard Rock Café in London by asking to place his guitar over his favorite seat. A free meal, appetizer or dessert on occasion will ensure they keep returning.

Alter suggestions. Since regulars may not open the menu, they may not be aware of new items or the daily special. Alter suggestions: "Since you normally order chicken, I thought I'd tell you about a new grilled chicken special you may want to try _____." Or: "The usual or would you like to try the _____." Or: "Did you know we also have _____."

Provide special treatment. Put regulars' pictures on the wall or keep pictures near the host stand so new hosts will know who to pamper. Also try these ideas:
- Introduce new servers to the regulars.
- Invite regulars in for tastings or to provide feedback on potential specials.
- Provide progressive discount cards — the more they dine, the more they save.
- Invite them to a focus group to find out what they like about your restaurant as well as competing restaurants.
- Make sure they know about your phone-ahead seating policy so they don't have to wait.
- Start a VIP program so cardholders get to bypass the wait or receive other special benefits and treatment.

©2010 pencom international · www.pencominternational.com

FIRST-TIME GUESTS

They're a blank slate. A tourist. Someone visiting on business. A newcomer to the area. Maybe they're responding to your advertising or heeding a referral from a friend or just dropping by. Win them over by delivering something better than ordinary.

How Can You Sizzle?

Recommend items you're famous for. "Since you've never been here before, you must try the _____." Or: "You just have to try our _____." Or: "You can't say you've been to _____ without trying the _____." Provide a small free sample of your signature item or dessert. Watch the register ring! First-time guests should get to experience things they cannot get anywhere else — your outstanding service and great food.

Provide direction. Instruct hosts to tell newcomers, during the seating process, where the restrooms are located. It's also a good time to talk about unique history, ambience and décor of the restaurant. If you have happy hour or other specials, let guests know.

Reassure selections. While it should be done for all guests, it's critical to let newcomers know they made the right choice:

> Guest: "I'll try the steak and shrimp special."
>
> Server: "Excellent choice. It's one of our most popular dishes."
>
> Guest: "I'll try the new draft beer."
>
> Server: "It's outstanding — you'll enjoy it!"

Talk to first-time guests. Introduce yourself and find out a little about them. Thank them for the opportunity to serve them and provide a bounce-back coupon for a future visit. A welcome from the manager is an added plus. Find out what you can do to get them to come back more often.

Action Item: Code the guest checks. Have hosts carry the guest checks and mark them with a star if they're seating newcomers. Then the server can customize the experience accordingly.

Pass the word along. Program a button on the POS system or put the tale number on a dry-erase board in the expo area that alerts the cooks, expediter and food runners. That way they know to make this dish and delivery extra special.

QUICK-MEAL GUESTS

Whether it's lunch or dinner, chances are (especially at lunch) guests may be in a hurry. Their main need? Speedy hospitality. Maybe they have to get back to the office or head out to a movie or show.

How Can You Sizzle?

Ask or look for cues. Do they appear to be in a hurry? (Example: They're ready to place the whole order the minute they sit down.) If unsure, ask: "You appear to be in a hurry — would you like me to have you in and out in no time?" Deliver the experience *they* want. Keep in mind that if you rush service and they're not in a hurry, you lose.

Recommend items that can be prepared quickly. If guests are in a hurry and someone orders a steak well-done or a difficult item to prepare, it's to their benefit (and yours) to let them know it will take a few extra minutes. They may want to change their choice if they feel it will take too long.

Drop the check. May seem like common sense, but is it common practice? Servers should be looking for cues, ready to drop and pick up the check at all times. If the credit card is at the table, it's time to show guests the total and process the payment immediately. Miss this step and all the good things done up to that point get diminished. When guests are waiting for the check, it's on their time — respect it. They're ready to go. Their need is speed!

Don't skip steps. There's a tendency to skip steps or force guests through all the steps in order in an effort to expedite the meal. It's better to combine or modify steps: Suggest dessert during the checkback. Take the complete order at the beginning if guests are ready. The steps are completed, just in a different order — the order guests want. Be unique. Suggest dessert to-go.

Now That's **Service That Sells!**

CASUAL-MEAL GUESTS

Not all guests want a fast-paced meal. Many want to relax and enjoy their time out, others want to be left alone while they work on business.

How Can You Sizzle?

Don't rush. Yes, these guests do slow down table turns, and it's hard to bite your lip and not be tempted to hurry them along. Some will want another cup of coffee or an after-dinner cocktail, while others will continue working or talking until they're ready to go. They key is don't rush.

Provide silent service. Don't forget about casual-meal guests. Servers should pay attention and deliver silent service, removing plates or glasses without interrupting the conversation. It's also important to make eye contact often. These guests will let you know if they need something.

Alter suggestions. Instead of viewing the table as a camper, servers can offer suggestions: "We feature outstanding after-dinner drinks and coffees — which sounds good to you?" Desserts or another round of drinks can be suggested in a similar fashion. If guests are hanging around, you might as well earn some money.

Keep serving. Refill coffee, iced tea or soft drinks throughout the course of the visit. Offer to box up leftovers. Servers should pick the opportune moments, not while guests are in the middle of conversation or a bite of food.

Taking care of casual diners requires patience. If outstanding service is provided, your restaurant will become the place of choice, whether it's to treat a hot date or launch a big business deal.

The goal overall is to drive frequency, to create regulars. To do so, match the service to guests' needs, modifying the steps of service if necessary. Regulars need a different set of suggestions than a first-timer. Guests in a hurry will till listen to a dessert suggestion, but it needs to be moved up and their check needs to be processed more quickly. Deliver "serve-us" service and your guests will be saying:

Now That's Service That Sells!

chapter four

CHAPTER 4

Which Path Am I On?

> Welcome back my friends to the show that never ends.
>
> We're so glad you could attend, come inside, come inside...
>
> Come inside the show's about to start
>
> Guaranteed to blow your head apart...
>
> *Rest assured you'll get your money's worth.*
>
> — Karn Evil No. 9
> Emerson, Lake and Palmer

Guests are lost by not properly executing the basics — food, service, cleanliness and atmosphere. If you don't provide these bare-minimum requirements, you're out of business. And, for the most part, restaurants do a satisfactory job. The basics, however, don't build loyalty. They're not unique. They don't sizzle.

It's time for the next step on the journey. Once guest frequency and speed have been determined, there are additional needs to take into consideration. The following groups fall into the categories discussed in the previous chapter (regulars, first-time guests, etc.) but they have additional needs:

- Families
- Value diners
- Celebrations and large parties
- Seniors
- Special-needs guests
- Guests with dietary concerns

chapter four

FAMILIES

There has been explosive growth in families dining out or ordering carryout because of two incomes and all the activities kids are involved in. Kids, in fact, continue to drive more and more decisions on where to eat. What restaurants are on the top of their list?

To illustrate the importance of addressing specific needs, a true story:

A family went out to a favorite casual-dining restaurant. The kids loved it because they had a coloring book for a menu and chips and queso to snack on. They'd been there so much, the kids didn't even open the menu to order. Shortly after the food arrived, the kids made it to the back page of the book and saw the menu — new items! Ribs ($2 more than the other kids' items) and a smoothie drink upgrade for 99 cents extra. Alas, it was too late as the food was already there. The family would have spent $6 more to feed the two kids what they wanted and now they were about to spend less and be unhappy about it. How easy was the fix? Simple. Had the host or server simply pointed out the new items, they would have added $6 to the top line of the company, and the guests would have been happier.

The service didn't match the needs. How many other products and programs have gone to the graveyard because of a lack of focus and execution? Focus on the needs of families.

How Can You Sizzle?

NOTE: This section is intended for restaurants where families represent a core group.

Pay attention. Extra napkins, kids' meals out early if parents agree, help with the kids, providing something to keep the kids busy. Be unique! Make them feel extra special.

Control the pace. Do parents want to eat quickly or enjoy a little relaxation?

Provide fun. What can occupy the kids? The more fun the experience is, the more often the family will return.

Train "kid focus." Many servers, hosts and other employees don't have children. Their frame of reference may be their pesky little sibling. Teach your staff how to talk to younger guests, including eye contact down at their level and compliments on coloring, eating or ordering. Here are some simple things younger employees or those without children might need to be taught: Don't put high chairs in high-traffic areas, don't place hot plates in front of small children and always put lids on drinks (or regret it later).

Make the restaurant kid-friendly. Try something different. Offer toys to play with at the table (an Etch-A-Sketch, for instance, or other small games). Let kids pick a toy on the way out (a la the dentist's office) or provide cool, interesting desserts or beverages (included in the price or for a slight up-charge). Consider: Push Pops, slushes, smoothies, etc. Create a wow for the kids to drive parents' loyalty.

Hit the "tweeners." As kids get to be seven or so, they outgrow kid's meals, but in many cases, Mom and Dad don't want to spring for the adult portion yet. Provide selections for the older child — more grown~up food, but smaller portions. Grilled chicken or fajitas, double-burgers, small steaks and rib baskets create a huge value statement for the restaurant.

Now That's Service That Sells!

chapter four

VALUE DINERS

Depending on the concept, there may be a fair share of guests looking for value, using coupons whenever possible or trying to get a deal. They may not appreciate a sales-focused approach, but their money counts the same. A dollar in the register is a dollar not in the competitor's. But how can you take care of these guests to make them feel special?

How Can You Sizzle?

Offer deals. What are the best ones you have on the menu? Let value diners know about them. Yes, they may not spend as much today and the tip may not impress, but they'll be returning again and again. It will pay off!

Alter suggestions. Put the information into value-friendly terms. For example:

- "The best value we have on the menu is the soup and salad."
- "For only $1 more, you can get a 22 oz. draft versus 14."
- "If you want to save a few dollars, the Chicken Nachos is a great appetizer to split."
- "I can bring out two forks so you can share the Chocolate Raspberry Cheesecake if you'd like."
- "Were you aware the entrées come with a salad and a vegetable? If you order a sandwich, the salad is $1.29 extra."
- "The best value is the combo platter — half portions of chicken and ribs."
- "You can get two pizzas for $15.99 or order one and save $5."

These simple suggestions can turn guests who used to be thought of as high-maintenance into ones singing praises of the restaurant. Make them feel good about getting deals.

CELEBRATIONS AND LARGE PARTIES

To guests celebrating an occasion or large parties, the only thing that matters is how the restaurant takes care of their special event. If 99.9% were good enough, 12 babies would be delivered to the wrong parents each day.

Expectations are much higher. Get it right! While celebrations may be obvious — reservations, packages or gifts coming in, etc. — others require a little work to uncover. "Celebration" is a broad term, covering a range of possibilities. Teach the staff to make these visits special.

How Can You Sizzle?

Ask: "What brings you in tonight?" This question can reveal clues to help wow guests. It's not just a birthday or anniversary you're looking for. Other reasons to celebrate include: job promotion, business deal, parents finding out they're expecting, house purchase, new to the neighborhood. When children are present, there's often a reason for the visit: graduation, report cards, lost a tooth, got a shot, went to the doctor, perfect dental checkup, moved up a belt in karate, finished a recital or play, and so on. Groups may be celebrating a going-away, sports team success or monthly get-together. Guests don't expect recognition for events such as these, but once discovered by the staff, the sky is the limit in creating a big splash.

Find out what type of recognition (if any) guests want. Some want public celebration (a birthday song from the staff, for example). Others don't feel comfortable standing on a chair wearing a sombrero. Guests may not want to make a big scene, but a cordial "thank you for choosing our restaurant to celebrate your special occasion" is a nice touch. Find out what *they* want!

Be prepared. Find out early on if there will be separate checks. No need for a fiasco at the end of the meal. Does the lead buyer want to make everyone feel comfortable in ordering anything off the menu? If so, servers should point out specials or suggest popular items. They should also ask for guests' attention to announce salad dressings, side-item choices, etc. If there's an automatic gratuity policy, let guests know up front. Deliver the service large groups require.

Set up the system. Program a celebration button onto the POS system. That way the kitchen, expediter and food runners can do something extra-special, and managers can visit the table and personally thank guests for celebrating with the restaurant instead of saying something generic like: "How's everything tonight?"

Have plenty of help. Many of the large-party guests may not have dined with you before. It's a prime opportunity to attract new business. Schedule plenty of help to run food, maintain tables, refill drinks and get re-orders. Minimize the dead time and wow all of the guests. They'll be back.

Throw in random acts of kindness. Examples: a sample of an appetizer or a free dessert. A ginger-ale toast for someone celebrating an anniversary or birthday, especially if children are present. When guests have a reservation, call them in advance to find out if they have any special requests or needs. Sizzle! Have their name on the table and be ready to greet them at the door. Use their name. If it's a recurring event (such as a book club or monthly employee lunch or meeting), confirm the next one. Call and follow-up the next day to see how everything went. It's not expected, but it's greatly appreciated and cements loyalty.

Guests who are celebrating have higher expectations than those just eating a meal. Don't let your staff give off the impression they're serving "just another table." Imagine parents in the delivery room ready to have a baby and the doctor acts like it's no big deal. How would they feel? When guests hear: "Thanks for allowing us to host your special occasion," *Now That's* Service That Sells!

SENIORS

Depending on the clientele, there may be quite a few seniors who dine at your restaurant. Their tendency as a group is to be loyal, but how can you satisfy their needs?

While at Chick-Fil-A one Saturday, I witnessed *Service That Sells!* at its finest. An elderly couple had a coupon for a free grilled chicken salad with the purchase of a large soft drink. The total was $1.69. How many places would think "cheap guests" and blow them off? After all, they really aren't helping build business that day. Heck, the store is probably losing money on the transaction.

Instead, sizzle happened: The lady asked for an extra plate to split the salad, and an extra cup to split the soft drink. Any typical restaurant would have given a hundred reasons why they weren't allowed to do that. After all, $1.69 for two people to eat? The cashier gladly gave them the plate and cup and the guests sat down to enjoy their meal. They felt like a million dollars and I've proceeded to tell this story to plenty of others. *Now That's* Service That Sells!

How Can You Sizzle?

Personalize service. Some seniors may want to chat, others may want to have a little privacy. If silent service is called for, deliver it. If guests are talkative, return the favor. Chances are, they'll be in every day.

Offer smaller portions. While there may not be an official seniors menu, provide off-the-menu meals with smaller portions, or allow seniors to split an entrée without an extra plate charge. Don't publicize smaller portion specials or splitting an entrée choice, but if guests inquire it's a great opportunity to create loyalty by making them feel special. Does it cost a little? Sure, but three visits per week at $12 per couple is worth more than $24 once a month. My grandmother was always loyal to places where she thought she was pulling one over on them. It was a small price for the restaurant to pay for a lifetime of loyalty and far cheaper than attracting new guests.

Avoid slang. Slang terms may not be understood or appreciated by seniors, or other guests for that matter. Stress the importance of respectful language. "Yes, ma'am or sir," "My pleasure" and "We'd be happy to" will make all the difference in the world. Talk to me, thank me, appreciate me. Phrases to avoid: cool, awesome, dude, like (as in, "It's like the best we have, dude"), fixin' to and still workin' on that. Provide the respect and treatment they desire.

SPECIAL-NEEDS GUESTS

Guests who are pregnant, need assistance getting around or are dining alone are an opportunity! Consider putting those folks at the top of the wait list. And treat them normally, even if you have to make a few special accommodations. Make them feel like every other guest — outstanding!

How Can You Sizzle?

Use common sense. If a guest is in a wheel chair, don't seat him or her in the main aisle the servers use. When leading the party to the table, ensure there's enough room to get through.

Take care of solo diners. Don't seat them in the middle of the restaurant where everyone can stare at them. Welcome them with something better than a scrunch-faced host who says, "Just one?" A better approach: "Will there be anyone else joining you tonight?" If paging the guest, leave off the "Party of one." A better approach: "Mr. Smith, your table is ready." Have a paper or magazines to read in case solo diners don't have one. Place them in a comfortable situation such as a side booth. Offer a community table where parties of one or two might choose to sit with others. It's a little more unique and inviting than the bar.

Set for success. Braille menus and room for wheelchairs or carts are simple items to have ready ahead of time for special-needs guests. See if they want to sit close to the restroom or an exit, or away from stairs if they have trouble or need assistance walking. ***Now That's*** *Service That Sells!*

GUESTS WITH DIETARY CONCERNS

Growing interest in low-carb diets and other fad diets, awareness of food allergies and food quality, and preoccupations with weight watching have created a new segment of guests demanding that you customize food to suit their needs. No longer are vegetarian options enough.

How Can You Sizzle?

Provide information. Guests want to know: Are there peanuts in this item? MSG? Animal enzymes? Is it kosher? How many grams of fat? Any desserts without sugar? Can I get a low-carb option? Ensure the staff is educated in these areas or at least knows where to go to find out the information. Creating an FAQ sheet or dietary-concern section on the POS terminal can be helpful. At your next meeting, conduct training on how to create low-carb options, or educate the staff on food allergies and prevalent dietary fads. Some of your competitors even arm servers with PDAs containing all dietary and food allergy information so they can immediately answer guests' questions. *Now That's* Service That Sells!

Be flexible. Guests want to be able to make special requests. If they're turned down, off they go to a more willing competitor. Special order charges frustrate guests. After all, if they order a burger with no bun, they are saving the restaurant money. Win some, lose some. Price it into the menu to minimize or eliminate up-charges.

Respect everyone. While employees may not agree with an expressed viewpoint at the table, they should respect it. Vegetarians should provide the experience meat eaters want — and vice versa. "The veggie burger is a popular alternative" works far better than, "I don't know, I prefer real meat patties."

Listen. Pay attention to special orders. Ask employees what they're hearing from guests with dietary concerns. Use the feedback to customize the menu or the training to address these needs. Encourage servers to ask if there are any special dietary concerns at the outset of the meal.

This chapter contains tons to digest, but it's the price of entry to compete today. "Serve-us," keep in mind, is the new expectation. "I want it my way at my price on my time." Variety is the spice of life. Servers won't be bored and guests will have a great time. The benefits of diversity have been talked about for a long time in regard to employees and the same holds true for guests. Celebrate the differences and reap the rewards. *Now That's* Service That Sells!

chapter five

CHAPTER 5

The Carryout Experience

Experience. Yes, that's correct — carryout needs to be an experience. Its surge and sales importance in the marketplace has forced many to remodel their restaurants to accommodate the business. But it has also fallen far short of many guests' expectations.

Guests order carryout for convenience. Dual incomes, kids' activities, low interest in cooking, no time — all have combined to provide a whole new revenue stream for many full-serve restaurants. As competition heats up in this arena, guests are becoming more and more demanding.

There are a few basics you must execute just to be in the game. Carryout does not mean fast-food service. It's not a drive-thru in most cases, is it? If the restaurant provides carryout service, the list of competitors expands to pizza-delivery chains and even QSR. The pool is large and ready to duke it out. Some are less expensive than others, some are closer to guests' homes, some deliver.

To shine, be better than the rest by providing an experience. It starts with the initial contact point — typically the phone. Has it been a critical part of guests' experience prior to the advent of carryout? Not really — it was simply used for directions, hours of operation, reservations and menu questions.

Now, it's a cash register. When guests vote with carryout dollars, their frame of reference is the pizza-delivery experience. Over the years, success in this world has been driven by interactive voice units to greet guests, messages while on hold, and service reps with huge amounts of POS-system data at their fingertips, including guests' order history, contact information, etc. To compete, there are new challenges never faced before.

> **To shine, be better than the rest by providing an experience.**

chapter five

PHONE

Answer it — guests are calling! Does the phone ring more than it ever did? Do you give it the training time and attention it deserves? The phone can make you plenty of money if handled properly. A few pointers:

Staffing. Is the phone staffed accordingly during peak times? The extra labor is easily justified by additional business and can be supplemented by strategic sales tips and suggestions. Or, do you have the bartender trying to answer the phone on a busy Friday night in addition to serving the bar guests and running the service bar? Save labor and lose sales— it's that simple.

Phone Skills Training. How is the phone answered? Think sizzle: "Thanks for calling _____ in _____, this is _____. May I help you?" Or: "_____, home of the best ribs and burgers, this is _____, may I help you?" Or: "_____. This is _____ and my favorite item on the menu is the _____. How may I help you?" If a guest calls inquiring about wait times and they're long, suggest carryout. Otherwise, the dollars go to competitors.

On-hold message. Use it as a sales-building tool. Record a message informing guests about specials, deals, upcoming events or features. Be unique. Direct guests to the web (assuming there's a menu online) or encourage them to fax in an order or offer to fax them a menu. Suggest items for the various diets out there.

Menu knowledge. In many restaurants, menu training for hosts and bartenders is an after-thought. Not a good idea if those employees are answering the phones and taking orders. They need to be prepared to answer questions, especially when guests don't have a menu in front of them. Do you want an order-taker or a money-maker?

Inform, don't sell. Let guests know about menu items that will enhance their experience. An order-taker who replies, "Anything else?" or "OK" at the end of an order, isn't driving business or service in the right direction. Teach phone-answering staff to reassure guests' choices and call attention to things they may have forgotten. Chapter 6 has more ideas on this subject.

The phone call can be a critical success factor in supporting marketing initiatives. How many times do people see advertising for a new product on the menu, but when they call to place an order, they forget about it? If the employee taking the call doesn't remind the caller about the new product, the restaurant misses out and

revenue is lost. The Army has a "don't ask, don't tell," policy — many restaurants have "don't ask, don't sell!"

A few other common-sense tips:

- Post directions from major intersections and landmarks by the phone.
- Quote accurate pick-up times.
- Provide a free soft-drink or iced tea if guests have to wait for their order (or suggest that they wait in the bar if they'd like a cocktail).
- Recommend a beverage for the road from the cooler.
- Suggest items that hold up better to-go. Face it, some foods just aren't meant to travel. Guests would rather hear a thoughtful recommendation versus getting the food home and it's a greasy mess. Example: "The nachos are outstanding, but they don't hold up well. Perhaps you'd like to try _____ instead. You'll be much happier." *Cha-ching!*
- Don't charge for to-go supplies such as bags, boxes, etc. Heck, restaurants save money if food is ordered to-go — minimal labor, reduced wait times, no silverware, plates or glasses to wash. Yes, there's a cost of the packaging, but guests aren't charged a separate fee to wash their dishes. Why charge extra for a box?
- No tip jars. They pressure guests, tend to be sloppy and appear unprofessional most of the time. If employees deliver out-of-the-ordinary hospitality, they'll still make money because most guests will, in fact, leave tips, and don't need a jar to encourage them to do so.
- Order from your restaurant on occasion. See if the to-go packaging works well. Soup or chili with a lid still may leak. Wrap containers with plastic wrap to keep seats and floor mats clean. Walk a mile in your guests' shoes.
- Large order? Something is going on. It may be a birthday party, some other kind of celebration, a group watching the big game or a book-club get-together. Find out what's going on and put a little wow into the carryout bag. Employees can ask: "Are you celebrating anything special?" If so, drop in a "happy birthday" or other appropriate note. If guests are watching a big game, drop in a "I hope your team wins." A child having a sleepover? Drop in a free kid's meal certificate for a future visit. *Now That's* Service That Sells!

> **No tip jars. They pressure guests, tend to be sloppy and appear unprofessional most of the time.**

Oce the order has been taken, the kitchen has prepared it and it's waiting for guests, **the carryout philosophy should be focused on 100% accuracy.** Your restaurant cannot afford to have guests get home and discover a mistake.

chapter five

THE PICKUP

Here are a few pointers to ensure guests have an outstanding experience when picking up their food. Again, seems simple, but these are key factors in determining whether or not guests order from you again (and how frequently).

- How do guests pick up their food? Is there a side entrance, staffed, with its own POS terminal, or do guests have to navigate through the busy waiting area and tell the host? If the host has to get the order and process payment, it takes too long and takes the host away from greeting and seating. Perhaps guests have to step up to the bar to pick up the order. How hard is it to flag down the bartender who's trying to tend bar, provide drinks for servers and maybe even serve the bar tables? Think carryout guests are top of the bartender's priority list? Be set up to succeed. The scenarios just mentioned limit your ability to generate sales. It's not convenient for guests. Imagine only one POS terminal at a quick-service restaurant. How busy would it be? Don't put a cap on sales. Have a dedicated pickup point staffed and ready.

- Check the order when bagging it and again when guests arrive, verbally confirming the order with them. Use clear bags and containers so items can be easily checked.

- What else do guests need? Utensils, condiments, napkins, etc. — all can be inquired about and provided before guests leave.

- Employees should also offer a to-go menu for next time. Guests typically don't have one when they call. They tend to order the same items over and over, or they request a faxed menu, which requires an additional call to place the order.

- Provide a coupon on the menu, with a short expiration date to encourage another order ... soon! Build frequency. Carryout is profitable, saves labor and eases the wait for tables during peak times.

- Thank guests and invite them back: "Thanks again, Ms. Smith. Look forward to seeing you next Friday."

What else could you do to distance your operation in the carryout race?

- Call back the next day or even a few hours later to find out how the meal was. You can't call everyone, but what a wow! Who else is doing this?
- Keep guests at the wheel. Many restaurants now deliver carryout food right to the car.
- Taking a page from the pizza-delivery business, keep a database of guests who order so you can contact them or track their habits. Send out fliers or cards to the most frequent guests. Drop a special offer to get those back who haven't dined with you in a while.

There's an opportunity to rise above the competition by providing *Service That Sells!* experiences to guests who choose to enjoy food at home.

Twenty years ago, nobody would have imagined fast-food restaurants would do over 60% of their business through their drive-thru. While carryout may be only a small percentage of your business today, it will continue to grow if executed properly. Every dollar in the cash register is one less to go to the competition.

chapter six

CHAPTER 6

Situational Selling

> S.A.L.E.S — Sell A Little Extra Something

Many guests are tired of pushy sales staff. Why? When suggestions are not made in the appropriate fashion or at the right time, they seem insincere and mechanical. It's been called "suggestive selling," "informing," "up-selling," "permission selling," and so on. It's evolved to "situational selling."

Sell what guests need to buy, not what the restaurant is trying to sell. The goal may be to sell as many Grande Appetizer Plates as possible, but many guests (parties of two or senior guests) would rarely buy it. So why ask everyone?

You've probably been out to lunch, dressed in business attire and received the "Anyone in the mood for a margarita?" suggestion. "Yes, I'm in the mood for a margarita, but I can't since I'm sitting here with my boss and we have to go back to the office to work!" Focus your energy and sales tactics in areas where you have the greatest chance of success. There is no one-size-fits-all answer.

The most common questions asked of servers are:

① What is the special?

② *What is good here?*

③ Where are the restrooms?

④ What would you recommend?

⑤ What is that table over there eating?

Situational selling can address most of these issues (along with help from the host on the restroom question). Before delving into specifics, take a look at the types of selling:

Types of Selling

Upselling

1. *Upselling* is enhancing an item already ordered (such as "up-sizing" a value meal or a draft beer, or adding cheese and guacamole to a burger).

Suggestive selling

2. *Suggestive selling* is describing an item guests have not ordered yet.

Situational selling

3. *Situational selling* is assessing the situation and *informing* guests of items or deals that best enhance that situation (let them make the choice).

Knowing why guests are paying a visit makes it easier to sell. Lose the monotone "Would you like to try our special today?" and insincere "I have to tell you about our soups or we get counted off by our mystery shopper," or "I'm trying to win a contest — would you like to buy a gift card?"

Is there any benefit to the guests in the previous situations? Suggesting enhancements to the meal is a key step in the cycle of service, but the practice needs to be subject to interpretation. While guests may not like to deal with pushy salespeople, there is no doubt they like to spend money and buy things they like or want. Make it easy for the guests to say yes.

 For example, regular guests may never open their menu. They know what they want. Can your servers skip the suggestion step? Sure, if you want to lose revenue!

Consider: A woman takes a client to her favorite local restaurant. Not needing to open the menu, she orders her usual meal. The client goes with the grilled chicken Caesar salad. "What? I didn't know that was on the menu. I'll have one of those also," the woman says.

Moral of the story: Alter suggestions to the situation: "Were you aware we now have a grilled chicken Caesar salad on the menu?" or "Since you like chicken, you may want to try the blackened chicken pasta special we have today. It's out of this world."

Another reason servers don't sell is they lack confidence. Why? They don't have enough knowledge. If, for instance, they don't drink wine or beer and haven't been trained well on these subjects (or the training was so long ago it's been forgotten), they're not likely to suggest these items. They're afraid they won't know an answer to guests' questions.

So what can be done to increase knowledge? Train them! Servers don't need to be experts on every ingredient and flavor profile, but they do need to be able to suggest items confidently and answer questions that guests may have. Simple ideas such as daily tastings, item-of-the-day discussions before the shift or recipe-card reviews will help the staff become more valuable to the guests and you!

Here are other ideas to help situational selling become a reality:

Ask questions. If guests can't decide which bottle of wine to order, an on-the-ball server can ask questions about what type of wine the guests usually like to drink and how much they prefer to spend. If they tend to gravitate toward inexpensive brands, it's wise to suggest something in their price range. Otherwise, they might suffer sticker shock at the end of the meal. Sell to the situation.

> **Servers don't need to be experts on every ingredient and flavor profile, but they do need to be able to suggest items confidently ...**

Suggest unique items. Everyone offers standard fare, and it should be on the menu, but to get guests coming back again and again, it's a good idea to let them know about items they can't get anywhere else. Or maybe it's the method of preparation that sets a familiar dish apart. In other words, promote what makes your food distinctive:

photocopying is prohibited

Server: "You may be thinking it's just another hamburger, but we cook ours over an open flame with mesquite and special seasonings. If you're not a meat-lover, you can order it with a veggie or black bean patty instead."

Modify suggestions to address specific dietary needs. Servers should find out if there are any dietary needs or concerns right up front: "Before I tell you about my favorites, does anyone have any dietary concerns or questions I can answer?" If they want a low-carb meal, suggest a low-carb beer or a glass of wine.

Watch what you say. When it comes to celebrations, determine who's paying. Is it OK to make suggestions about specials or is there a price range in mind? Work with the party host to identify parameters and customize suggestions.

Follow the lead. During business meetings, guests often hesitate to order an appetizer, dessert or alcohol. Servers can usually identify the person in charge and take his or her order first. If an appetizer or, say, a beer is ordered at that point, others will follow suit. On the other hand, if the top dog goes last, chances are a bunch of waters with lemon will be heading to the table. Another approach is to discreetly ask the person in charge if it would be appropriate to suggest items such as beer or wine.

Eliminate questions such as "Would you like..." and "Do you want..."
They virtually encourage a "no" response. For example, "Would you like dessert?" If guests are indecisive, "no" is the easy way out. Or perhaps they'll decline because there are too many unanswered questions: "How much is it?" and "What do you have?" and "Which one is the best?"

When you don't make it easy for guests to see the benefits, expect "no." What's more, the proper answer to "What's good here?" is never "Everything." Guests want direction. What are they in the mood for? What type of meal are they looking for (pasta, salad, steak)? Information is power. Power to deliver *Service That Sells!*

Watch the negatives. Since most servers only sell like they've been sold to, they tend to repeat what they hear when they eat out. Unfortunately, many of those phrases are negative and may have crept into their vocabulary. When was the last time you actually listened to one of your servers or hosts make suggestions? Post a sign in the break area or on the POS terminal with a big red X through these phrases:

> "You don't want dessert (or an appetizer or another beer) do you?"
>
> "Anything else?"
>
> "Decided yet?"
>
> "Is that all?"

Offer a choice of two. Servers should use "Which would you prefer?" instead of "Would you like...?" It's not selling as much as it is informing guests of their choice and letting them decide. For example:

Beer

> Guest: "I'll have a draft beer."
>
> Server: "We have two sizes of draft, 16 and 22 oz. Which would you prefer?"

Wine

> Guest: "I'll have a chardonnay."
>
> Server: "The house chardonnay is _____ and we also feature _____ and _____. Which sounds good to you?"

Alcohol

> Guest: "I'll have a vodka tonic."
>
> Server: "Which type of vodka do you prefer? Our well vodka is _____ and we also offer _____ and _____."

Desserts

> Guest: "What do you have for dessert?"
>
> Server: "Are you chocolate lovers?"
>
> Guest: "Yes!"
>
> Server: "We have a chocolate mountain cake and a chocolate mousse truffle. Both are ideal for sharing. Which should I bring out — or should I bring them both out?"

Inform guests about favorites or features. Pointing out value can be helpful, too. Sell the benefit to guests. Let them buy what they want, not what you're trying to sell. Effective phrases are:

- "John is in the kitchen tonight and his specialty is _____."
- "My favorite chicken dish is the _____."
- "The most popular beers we sell are …"
- "If you're really hungry I'd recommend the _____."
- "Were you aware we also serve _____?"
- "Did you know tonight's feature is _____?"
- "The best deal is _____."
- "The last expensive way to do that is _____."
- "If you want to splurge on this happy occasion, I'd suggest _____."
- "If it were me, I'd get the _____."
- "If you want low carbs, may I suggest the _____."
- "If you're looking for something low-cal, the best tasting item would be the _____."
- "You may not realize we offer some 'bigger kids' meals which are actually smaller portions of our fajitas or rib baskets."
- "If you want to save a few dollars, you can order the half-rack and chicken combo. It's still a lot of food and leaves room for the dessert I heard you mention."
- "The best meals under $15 would include _____."

Remind staff to say it in guests' terms. Suggesting the best deal to value-conscious guests is ideal but may be offensive to those wining and dining a party. If they want to splurge, let them! When going through the car-buying process, the salesperson usually puts buyers into a fully loaded model, then removes things not wanted. More often than not, the buyers spend more money than planned, but feel like they saved money because things were eliminated.

The same can work for a restaurant: Package an appetizer, two entrées and a dessert to split at a slight savings (as an off-the-menu special to test). Guests go for the deal, save a few cents (but spend more than planned), and the server doesn't have to be pushy. It's a win for guests, the server and the restaurant.

Suggest dessert to go. Face it, with the large portion sizes of most restaurants, guests typically don't buy dessert, and many servers would rather turn the table than have guests remain for another 15 minutes (and an additional $1 tip). The answer? Offer dessert to-go. *Now That's* Service That Sells!

Keep score. Retail chains routinely post sales check averages, as well as the highest total sales on a quarterly or annual basis. Imagine your servers' faces when they see their total sales for the year are over $100,000 or they have the top check average in the store, district or whole chain. Information is power — the power to deliver *Service That Sells!*

Situational selling is based on the confidence to guide guests to yes. Success requires training. There's an old story about a couple of shoe salespeople who get sent to a remote area to sell shoes to the tribes people. The first salesperson calls in to the supervisor and says: "No opportunity here — nobody wears shoes." The second salesperson calls in to the supervisor and says: "An incredible opportunity here — nobody wears shoes!" *Now That's* Service That Sells!

chapter seven

CHAPTER 7

The Manager (That's You!)

> It's the singer, not the song
> that makes the music move along.
>
> "Join Together with the Band"
> — The Who

Face it, most restaurants provide decent food, fair prices, OK service and an average atmosphere. So what truly separates one from another? Take a look in the mirror, baby. **It's the manager on duty — *you!* — who makes the biggest difference.**

You determine if employees look sharp. You set the tone and expectations of service. So ask yourself: Do you run the shift or does the shift run you? Do you make it happen, watch it happen or wonder what happened?

Chain restaurants have numerous locations with the same building design and menu, similar people and advertising. Yet some run better than others. Why? The manager on duty (M.O.D.).

Managers, owners, franchisees — all make shifts happen! To drive change effectively, it's wise to exaggerate the actions needed. Think about how hard it is to start pedaling a bike. Moving a gear initially takes extra effort but becomes easier as it gathers momentum. The same holds true when moving your staff in a new direction. Create the buzz and the energy. Get the staff primed for the show and keep it revved up the entire time.

Leading the charge and setting the example are the first steps.

If the team isn't improving every day, the competition is catching up or passing by. There are numerous sizzle points managers can execute with guests. In most restaurants, if managers interact with guests at all, it's at the table.

Typical Table Visits

- Mechanical, robotic and scripted.
- Disinterest in what guests are saying.
- Hovering over the table.
- Questions asked are general: "How is everything?"

If guests respond "Alright" or "OK," are those answers acceptable? Many of your competitors think so. Parts of the visit may be great, others average and some not so good. When they're all rolled up, they're merely "OK." Managers learn nothing but feel good because they hear no complaints about what's really happening.

Service That Sells! Table Visits

- Questions asked are specific.
- "Are your entrées outstanding?"
- "Is _____ taking excellent care of you tonight?"
- Bring a pitcher: "May I refill your water?"
- "I see you ordered tonight's special. Is it better than expected?"
- The bartender has your beer ice cold when you are ready for another!"
- "I understand it is your first time here. What brought you in?"
- "How did you find out about us?"
- "Where else do you dine? What do they do better?"
- Anything we can do to provide a better experience?"
- "What could we do to get you in more frequently?"
- "Thanks for choosing us to celebrate. Are we taking great care of you?" "Did we do anything outstanding today?"
- Eye contact made with guests, perhaps down at their level.
- Children get complimented (how they color, how well they ate, how they did in their game today if they are wearing a uniform).
- Responses and cues listened for: OK is not OK.

Now That's Service That Sells!

An effective manager truly values guests' business, personally demonstrating that they're not just a number or a step on a checklist. When running the pulse check in your own operation, rub elbows with guests at multiple points and look for opportunities to wow them.

Working the Lobby

- "Glad to see you"
- "Just a few more minutes. Believe me, it will be worth the wait!"

Thanking Departing Guests

- "I'll be working Tuesday through Saturday next week. Let me know when you're coming in again. You have to try our weekday specials!"
- "We appreciate you coming in tonight! What was your favorite item?"
- "See you tomorrow!"

In the Bar

- "Do you like the new drink specials — the large drafts are a great deal, aren't they?"
- "Is _____ making the best drinks in the city?"
- "Don't forget about the half-price appetizers."
- "Next time don't forget to try the _____ on tap."

Meals Not Eaten

- "Was the dish not prepared to your liking?"
- "May I get you something else?"
- Fix the problem or take it off the bill.

At the Table

- Have a purpose and reason to be there. Find out information to help drive business.
- Refill drinks.
- Remove plates or glasses. For example, "Are you still enjoying the _____ or may I remove your plate?"
- Offer to box leftover food.
- Find out how their service is.
- Promote specials or marketing initiatives currently going on.
- Provide a bounce-back coupon.

- Invite guests in for special events (wine tastings and classes, samplings of specials, focus group feedback).
- Have guests fill out a contact card to be mailed or e-mailed specials and coupons.
- Have any employees gone out of their way to help out?
- What else can we do to build frequency?
- Where else do the guests eat? Why? What does the competition do better?
- Any part of the visit just OK or ordinary?

Table visits tend to be an interruption of guests' meals. Use the time instead to build sales and relationships. Along the way, you'll minimize the big complaints. And, if an experience does fall short and you've already visited the guests, they won't be as angry.

Guests, in fact, often want to make management "aware of something" versus "complaining." You will hear more feedback if the guests know you care. Rather than walk out, never to return, they present the opportunity to resolve the situation. A little thing at first could become a big thing if left unaddressed.

Speaking of complaints, everything doesn't always come up roses. There'll be times when guests simply aren't satisfied. Remember, the competition is shooting for "satisfied" and is happy with "OK." In your world, falling a little short of "outstanding" is far better than reaching "OK." When the guests let you know of an issue, do you view it as an opportunity to sizzle or cringe at the sound of another complaint?

Typical Responses to Odd Requests or Complaints

- "No."
- "Can't do that."
- "Only if you pay more."
- "It's our policy."
- "You don't have a reservation."
- "We don't take reservations."

Service That Sells! Responses

- "Yes, for a small additional charge we would be happy to do that."
- "Another way to do that would be..."
- "The best way to ensure you are seated quickly is..."
- "What I can do for you is..."

Now That's Service That Sells!

Employees' responses must be positive. Yet they typically don't know how to do it when they begin working. Why? When they dine out, they're treated negatively. Managers must model and train the desired behaviors. If they don't practice this philosophy, the employees certainly won't. Look in the mirror — do you believe it? Are you passionate about it?

A steak chain has a sign featuring the alphabet with the "N" and "O" crossed out. "NO isn't spoken here!" Guests don't like hearing what they can't have or what's not possible.

a b c d e f g h i j k l m ⊗ o p q r s t u v w x y z

Empower your employees to respond properly to any kind of request. To be successful, they'll need the training and the autonomy to make good decisions. You'll need to support them, even if they make mistakes from time to time. In those cases, it's wise to discuss the matter privately, never in front of guests. A good way to start: "What could we have done differently to prevent the situation from occurring?"

Employees who can solve problems and know they have the backing of management will provide great service. Fries are cold? Drink is wrong? Steak is under-cooked? Employees can take care of these situations. If the manager has to get involved, use this acronym:

chapter seven

L.E.A.S.T.
Listen, Empathize, Apologize, Solve, Thank

Listen.

Many guests simply want to vent their frustrations and know that someone has heard them.

Empathize.

Not sympathize ("I feel bad for you"). Empathize ("If that happened to me, I'd also be upset"). Repeat back the issues to guests to make sure they're understood.

Apologize.

Many times "I'm sorry" will make the problem all better. When the restaurant falls short of expectations, guests deserve an apology.

Solve.

Fix the problem. Many managers try to buy guests off. An insincere comp, however, won't cut it if guests don't feel like the problem is solved. Example: "I'm sorry we were out of toilet paper, here's a coupon for a free dessert." The freebie won't be used if guests don't return.

Thank.

Thank guests for bringing the situation to light. It's an opportunity to build loyalty. Thousands of people leave restaurants each day unhappy and never return. Silence isn't golden!

Hospitality expert Jim Newberry suggests using the "complaint-o-meter." Judge complaints on a scale of 1 to 10 — always from the guest's point of view. A hair in food may be a 2 to you, but a 10 to the guest. If you act like it's no big deal, the meter could run up to 20. Once you ascertain the level of the complaint you can provide the proper resolution.

Judge complaints on a scale of 1 to 10 — always from the guest's point of view.

Items lower on the meter (in the eyes of the guest) can usually be resolved with immediate action, listening, apologizing and manager involvement. Out of toilet paper in the restroom? Apologize and fix it. Buying their steak doesn't solve the problem. An under-cooked steak, on the other hand, can be quickly fixed.

Items in the middle of the meter require compensation. An overcooked steak cannot be quickly fixed and the guest will not be eating while the rest of his or her party is. Deducting the meal off the bill, a free meal for a future visit or a free dessert are good options.

Complaints on the high end of the meter — rude employees and foreign objects in food, for example — may require a full comp ... *plus!* Don't stop until guests say: "No you don't have to do that. Really, that's enough."

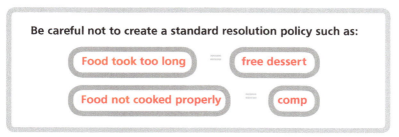

And so on. It should be clear by now that every guest and every situation is different.

Guests don't want you to disrespect their time. Even providing a refund for a 10 on the complaint-o-meter may not be enough for two hours of wasted time and a ruined evening out. Be unique and ensure the situation is resolved to their satisfaction.

Additionally, leave the P&L out of the equation. Comping a dinner may seem like it cost the $15 menu price, but, in actuality, it was $5 worth of food. Providing a

chapter seven

free meal on a future visit doesn't cost the full retail value — only the actual cost of items provided.

> **There'll always be a small percentage of guests out to scam you. The vast majority, though, want to spend money.**

There'll always be a small percentage of guests out to scam you. The vast majority, though, want to spend money. So, the next time guests claiming to have a reservation pitch a fit when they're not on the list, go ahead and give in. They want to spend money — let them! Guests using an expired coupon — it's OK. No attitude from employees, just a simple "My pleasure." The guests will be back and more loyal than ever! *Now That's* Service That Sells!

The last — and quite large — piece of the managerial puzzle is profitability. Volumes have been written on the subject to help save a nickel here and there. The focus has been bringing in the dollars. No sense regurgitating a bunch of well-worn rhetoric on dumpster dives and trash digs for silverware.

Let's aim the thought process on the largest controllable expense — labor. Yes, cutting labor has an immediate short-term impact on the bottom line, and there are plenty of right times and reasons for managers to make the call. Trying to deliver *Service That Sells!* may seem costly at first blush and initial reactions from district managers and area supervisors may be: "Not this month." Look at it from a different angle before rushing to a decision.

There are two ways to increase profitability: raise sales or lower expenses. In many cases, labor expense needs to be adjusted down. But what if you want to add hours to the schedule to enhance service levels? First, see where labor hours are not needed and can be re-allocated to more productive times. If there's still a need for more hours, look at two things:

Check averages. If all the best servers and bartenders were working on the same shift (ideally the busiest ones), how much higher would sales be than what the current team of servers and bartenders is producing? If the restaurant serves 250 guests during a dinner shift and runs a check average only 50 cents higher, $125 in additional sales is generated. The additional sales keep labor in line (or even lowers it) while keeping the restaurant fully staffed to provide wow experiences for guests who, in turn, will return more frequently.

Return on investment. If staff needs to be added to ensure *Service That Sells!* happens, let everyone know how much sales must be increased to provide the ROI necessary to compensate for the additional labor.

Example:

Let's say that hosts or bartenders execute carryout service and phone answering. Sales and service levels are adequate, at best. You want to add personnel to answer the phone quicker and provide better carryout service during the dinner rush, which would free up hosts and bartenders to focus on dine-in guests. To cover the peak hours, two additional employees are necessary. Hourly labor typically runs at 18%. What additional sales must be generated to justify the labor?

How do two carryout employees make up the $194? Simply answering the phone may drive incremental sales. If guests get placed on hold or the phone rings and rings, the calls may go to a competitor. Having employees trained and dedicated to carryout service also enhances suggestive-selling opportunities.

What if the additional carryout sales for the night are only $180? Is the program ineffective? Don't forget the additional sales and service enhancements provided by the bartenders and hosts who were previously bogged down with to-go orders. If the bartenders' sales increase as a result of having dedicated carryout personnel, those dollars should also be figured into the mix.

There'll likely be a skeptic reading this who says: "Why would I want to have my labor go up?" The additional revenue generated raises top-line sales. Increasing top-line sales lowers the cost percentages per line, as well as raises the profit percentage flowing to the bottom line. Even if sales fall slightly short of goal and labor increases .1%, the additional sales will lower all the other cost lines to ensure the right financial decision is made.

Selling desserts or extra cheese on pizzas raises the food cost line. Should those items not be suggested? If you focused on food cost, you wouldn't want these items sold. Looking at the big picture, however, you can see overall sales increasing as well as profits. Fixed cost items such as salaries, utilities, etc., remain the same whether the item is sold or not, so they decrease on a percentage basis, hence the overall profitability increase.

Don't take the managerial eye off cost controls. Do, however, open up the focus on how building sales helps increase margins and lower costs. Otherwise, ineffective business decisions are made. The old saying "Don't trip over dollars to pick up pennies" says it best. Focus on the top line, train the front line, and the dollars will be on the bottom line.

Let's take a look at the front line.

chapter eight

CHAPTER 8

The New Players

> Hire me, train me, reward me, retain me.

It's a simple mantra to guide your management of human resources, but what goes wrong? Lack of a top line, too much focus on the bottom line, ignoring good employees, allowing slackers to stay, bad hires, inadequate training, no recognition or appreciation — all of these factors lead to turnover.

To help unravel and solve this mystery, let's start at the beginning.

There are **four key components** to creating a successful team:

1. Who you hire.
2. How you train them.
3. Who trains them.
4. The environment they work in.

chapter eight

Old hat? Yesterday's news? Common sense? Retro is back and it's cool. There's a new spin on the old favorites. It used to be slow and boring, but now it's hip, cool, upbeat and geared toward today's employees.

Let's look at each part, starting with hiring. Everyone's heard that hiring is the most important thing you do as a manager. It's more than that. Hiring the *right person* is the most important thing you do.

Book after book has been written about hiring, and many companies provide pre-employment testing (Pencom International www.pencominternational.com), computer kiosk applications and background checks. While those items certainly help make the right decisions, they're only a piece of the puzzle. So what else can you do?

First, know what to look for. What are the requirements of each position in the restaurant and the skills necessary to do the job? Most restaurants have job descriptions and use them to frame their interview questions.

To take it one step further, assess what skills the best employees have. Ask employees to write down what they do and the skills necessary to excel.

Why are they more successful and productive than others? Talk to them to find out why they believe they produce the results they do. Find those same skills and traits in your new hires.

Drill down to specifics. It's not enough to say we need "friendly, outgoing, energetic people." Who doesn't? Most companies' job descriptions for a server, host or line cook look pretty similar. What's the difference between the great and the not-so-great? Usually it's a manager's ability to assess and uncover these skills in an interview.

> **Interviews should be thought of as auditions. Have applicants demonstrate the skills necessary versus nodding their head "yes" or "no" to your questions.**

Many companies today teach managers how to interview as well as provide the specific questions for managers to ask. It's not the questions, however, that matter the most. It's the answers.

So what skills do employees who can deliver *Service That Sells!* possess? What is their service DNA? All the common ones you could name quickly: outgoing, friendly, hospitable, like to serve others, and so on. But what else do they need?

Keep in mind that an applicant's frame of reference for the duties of a host, server or bartender is the restaurant up the street.

If part of the job description of a host is to show guests to their table, anyone can do that. However, if you want a host to describe the special or find out why guests are visiting, it requires a different skill set.

Interviews should be thought of as auditions. Have applicants demonstrate the skills necessary versus nodding their head "yes" or "no" to your questions. Ask yourself, too, what specific talents are needed for each position — the intangibles, traits or skills possessed by your great employees. A few to consider:

HOSTS

Continuous movement or action.

Seating is an integral part of the job, but getting out from behind the stand to make greetings is key. Do guests want the first impression to be an unenthusiastic person leaning against a door or holding the stand down? Find people who want constant motion. During slow times they can assist with drink refills, clean the entry floors and glass or help with to-go orders. **Sample interview questions:** What do you do when it's not busy? What is a typical day like? What do you do when there is nothing to do? At your previous job, show me how you greeted guests. Hosts need to be able to handle stress with a smile!

Double-dose of personality.

Look for applicants who can turn on the charm to welcome guests and speak energetically about the restaurant and its food while escorting guests to the tables. Interview strategy: **Have applicants role play** taking you to a table. If they can't do a great job during the interview, they certainly shouldn't be allowed to seat guests for real.

Lasting impressions.

Hosts are often responsible for first and last impressions, yet they may spend only five to 10 seconds with guests (longer if they're seating them). Can your host applicants wow in a short time? How do they interact and talk? Can they smile? Are they outgoing? Do they have the potential to make great first impressions, including a professional appearance and the ability to build rapport with guests? Eye candy goes only so far. Interview strategy: **Have applicants greet you as if you were a guest** just walking up to the host stand. Also have them review your restaurant's dress code and ask if they have any questions or comments.

SERVERS

Sales skills.

Do applicants have what it takes to sell? Interview strategy: Have them role play selling a specific item. Ask how they would rate past service experiences, as well as how they would improve them. Sample questions: What are your monetary needs per week? How do you feel you can help achieve those needs? How would you suggest an appetizer? Sell me your favorite item (from a previous job or what they like when they dine out).

Detail oriented.

Taking care of details is the name of the game. Interview strategy: Watch a server taking care of a guest and ask applicants to provide feedback on what they see. Do they know specifics and standards? Do they focus on little things? What did the server do right? What could have been done better?

Greeting.

Can server applicants make a wow from the outset? Interview strategy: Have them approach and greet you as they would one of their tables. Would you want this person taking care of you? Look for smiles, eye contact and enthusiasm.

Multi-tasking.

Good servers received an extra dose of this gene. Look for applicants who are involved in numerous activities and jump from one thing to another. Servers have to juggle many things at the same time. Sample questions: What do you do when there is nothing to do? Did you like the last job better when it was busy or slow? Why? What other duties did you have?

chapter eight

 A few tips on the interview itself:

- Be as interactive as possible. It's an audition, after all. Use plenty of what-if situations and have applicants demonstrate skills.
- Have key employees sit in on interviews and give feedback. What did they see? Would they want this person on their team?
- Have key employees give applicants a brief tour of the restaurant and talk about some specifics of the job. This time can be used to get a better gauge on applicants in an informal setting.
- Invite applicants to have a meal in the restaurant and, afterward, conduct a detailed assessment to see how observant they are about service levels.
- Don't hire applicants who have to be sold on taking the job. You shouldn't have to sell to them, they should be marketing their skills to you.
- Follow all legal requirements for interviewing.

The staff should be a reflection of your guest base, not carbon copies of you. A football team with 11 quarterbacks wouldn't be very successful. Fill the needs of the team. Keep in mind, too, that outgoing performers on-stage are often the quiet ones off-stage.

Don't get too caught up with the application itself. It's two-dimensional. Applicants are three-dimensional. And, bottom line, guests don't care about applications. They do care about being served by outstanding people with personality and sizzle. Interview, audition and role-play — then select the best.

Once your superstars are on-board, it's time to gear them up to provide *Service That Sells!* It begins at orientation. Many of you are thinking, "yuck — orientation!" Is your orientation a 90-minute policy-a-thon consisting of the following items?

Typical Orientation

- Listen to a monologue from an unenthusiastic manager.
- Paperwork, paperwork, paperwork.
- Read the mission statement (which means little to new employees).
- Sit down with a long, boring handbook.
- Endless policies and procedures.
- Find out all the things you can and cannot do.
- Any questions? (Of course not, they're still too intimidated.)

Sounds like a trip to the principal, not a "Welcome to the team!"

Service That Sells! Orientation

- Fun, upbeat welcome and introduction to the staff — it's the first day of a new career!
- Review benefits, payroll, schedules, training program, etc.
- Start on a high note — all the great things about working at the restaurant.
- Cover history, positions, common terms and a bit on profitability (so they understand where all the money goes).
- Take a thorough store tour, leading a "walking classroom." (In other words, don't plant new hires in a booth or leave them alone for 20 minutes to watch a video.)
- Review employee responsibilities (uniform, parking, guidelines).
- Cover the *Service That Sells!* philosophy and employees' roles in the success of the business. (If this topic is not covered on day one, it will be perceived as unimportant.)

Now That's Service That Sells!

chapter eight

Sizzle employees and they'll sizzle guests. To ensure consistent orientations, create color slides or flipcharts for managers to use and new hires to follow along. Whenever possible, involve star employees. They can lead tours, provide insights into the training program and talk about what it's like to work at the restaurant. Employees listen to peers more than managers. Establish a partner for new hires to go to with questions they may not want to ask superiors.

Orientations set the tone for the whole employment experience. Make yours interactive, seeking two-way communication every step of the way. A week or two afterward, conduct a "post-training orientation," during which you can find out if new hires have any questions now that they've been around a while. You can also solicit feedback about their training experience to date.

Next step, training. Airlines spend 14 hours of maintenance for every one hour of flying time. Are employees so lucky? Or is it, "Oh, great, another week of wearing a stupid 'trainee' nametag and shadowing another employee who really doesn't want to help or even know what he or she is doing."

Lose the "trainee" nametags. Guests don't care if an employee is new. They just want outstanding service. If guests were asked to rate a training program, how would they view its effectiveness? Solely based on the service they received.

Focus your training efforts on the items of importance to guests. Train on hospitality, not just tasks.

Focus your training efforts on the items of importance to guests. Train on hospitality, not just tasks. Small details and nuances can be taught over time. Don't cram so much information into trainees' heads that they lose sight of what really matters or forget everything they've learned. Watch kids learn how to play a computer game. They don't read the manual, they figure it out by practicing and asking questions when needed. People learn differently so vary the methods — a mix of manuals, videos, job shadows, quizzes, skill assessments, role plays and plenty of practice!

Training typically is thought of like school. Schools educate you. Education is providing knowledge and information. Guests don't care about knowledge and information unless it translates into action. Training focuses on skills and behaviors.

Think about learning to drive. Step one is education (class, video, reading, tests) followed by training (on-the-road practice). A qualified instructor runs the show until the driver proves he or she is ready. The final leg is a demonstration of ability and a written test to obtain the coveted license. Are restaurant employees trained in this fashion? The downside to 'driver's ed?' Everyone is treated the same way, no matter what their experience. Just as you need to customize the guest experience, you also need to customize the training experience.

Today's employees live in a digital world. They have been hit from all angles since the day they were born. They watch TV (the news channel with video, weather, sports scores and stock prices all on the same screen at once). At the same time, they can have an online chat (or 6), listen to the stereo, talk on their cell phone, play a video game and do their homework all at the same time. VHS? Boring.

Think T.O.D.
training on demand

Give employees what they need to know right now. Later, give them what they need to know then. They function like DVD, skipping around to see only the parts they want to see at a given time.

Have a large menu? Train the top 20 items guests order (it's probably more than 80% of your sales). Ensure employees know those 20 items forward and backward. Follow up over the next few weeks to ensure they learn the remaining items as well.

Set up your training in "buckets" three to 10 minutes long — covering only those items needed at that point. Don't subject employees to the whole program just because "it's the program."

chapter eight

Typical Training Program

- Read a boring manual, sit in a two-hour class or watch a long video.
- Cram tons of information into a short window of time.
- Focus on mechanics and steps.
- Get sent home early when it's slow to save labor.
- Follow someone around who may or may not follow standards.
- Pore over every last detail, even if it doesn't matter to guests.
- Memorize a bunch of stuff to pass a test (then forget it).
- Jump too quickly into a position and sink.
- Training, what's that?

Sound familiar? If so, here are a few suggestions:

Service That Sells! Training Program

- Participate in rapid-fire changing of methods — small manuals or cards with bulleted information and lots of photos intermixed with role-plays, short classes and bursts of video for the initial portion of the day.
- Apply what was just learned by practicing as long as necessary.
- Enjoy a self-paced learning environment, moving on to the next step only after "getting" the previous one.
- Focus on hospitality and soft-skills — how you say things, body language and providing outstanding service to guests — role play on the trainer, not the guest!
- Complete daily reviews and skill assessments, which also ensure trainers are on track.
- Work with trainers who have been validated to train and follow standards.
- Learn the main components of guest service and the job first, including key menu items. The rest will come down the road.
- Expect 30/90/180-day re-validations of skill and knowledge.

Now That's **Service That Sells!**

So how do trainers get selected and prepared? What process do they go through to get certified? If their only frame of reference is how they were trained, they may not be equipped to succeed and the cycle of training shortcomings will continue.

Try this exercise at your next trainer's meeting. Ask for a volunteer, then set the scene: "A barefoot alien has landed in the yard and desperately needs a pair of shoes. I'll pretend I'm the alien and, not knowing a thing about putting on and lacing up shoes, I'm going to follow your instructions exactly."

> **You've tied your shoes thousands of times, but teaching another person to do it is difficult.**

The volunteer may have no idea of where to start or where to go. Others in the group may pitch in an idea or two. Whatever the instruction, it's bound to be clumsy. You've tied your shoes thousands of times, but teaching another person to do it is difficult.

What matters? Getting the shoes tied. Yet folks involved in this exercise will often disagree about the "right way" to proceed. The point is that there are many right ways to tie shoes. Don't argue about how to get there — just focus on the end result.

Trainers need to be certified in the same fashion as new employees. Candidates should shadow a certified trainer in action, watching how he or she trains each topic. The trainer should ask questions to reinforce information, and "lengthen the leash" to let the trainee gradually take on more responsibility, even in the face of a mistake or two. That's how people learn.

Typical Trainer Certification

- "You're my best employee — new you're a trainer. Get busy."
- "You've been here six months — now you're a trainer."
- "The trainer called in sick. Go train the new person." ("But I've only been here a week!")
- "Go to this class (or read this manual) and you will be certified."
- "I know you don't do it that way, but it's what the book says, so show them the right way."
- "The new employee has to be in full uniform, so do you."
- "Just let them follow you around and show them everything you do."
- "Do it because it's what the book says."
- "Training is *somebody else's* responsibility."

Service That Sells! Trainer Certification

- Qualified candidates are given assignments to test ability and commitment. Example: They could create a small training module to reinforce hosts' menu knowledge.
- They learn how to deliver feedback and coach employees, using available resources (classes, books, videos) and role-plays to gain comfort with the process.
- They shadow an existing trainer to see how it's done.
- They learn the ins and outs of "classroom" training, starting with short classes such as menu knowledge, service delivery and register procedures.
- They use a leader's guide or daily checklist of activities for the trainer to cover.
- They understand the "why" behind the standards and can explain them to trainees.
- They learn to monitor the success of new employees long after initial training is complete.
- "Training is *everyone's* responsibility."

Now That's Service That Sells!

Once there's a certified training team in place, managers need to validate the skills of new employees:

Typical Skill Validation

- "What's a skill validation? They passed the test — they're ready."
- "You know how to suggestively sell, don't you?"
- "You know how to greet the guest, right?"
- "You were trained in all these areas, right?"
- "Did you read the manual?"
- "Did you watch the video?"

Service That Sells! Skill Validation

- There's a checklist of skills to assess.
- New employees demonstrate the appropriate skills to do their jobs.
- Manager provides feedback — not jus saying what they did right, but finding out how they think they did versus what they wanted to do during each skill validation. Finally, what would they do differently next time? Ensure the trainee is ready to serve your guests.
- Action plan is developed to follow up on additional training needs.
- Trainers also receive feedback on their performance.

Now That's Service That Sells!

chapter eight

- **Hire me**
- **Train me**
- *Reward me*
- *Retain me*

✱

Two parts down. The staff has been hired and trained. Now they're taking care of guests — or are they? And what about existing staff?

chapter nine

CHAPTER 9

Leading the Revolution

> Serve 'em like an all-star and treat 'em like a guest star.

Training new employees is the simple part of the equation. In fact, opening a new restaurant — from a training perspective, at least — is ideal. There are no unwanted habits, preconceived notions or bad apples.

For most managers, however, there's an existing base of employees who need to be re-energized, re-focused and re-trained. Is it *re-diculous*? How do you get them to buy in to the new way? They've heard it all before. Most ignore it and, a few days later, it's back to business as usual.

benefits

The first step in convincing employees to embrace change is to describe the benefits. Try these two on for size:

short-term

In the short-term, their enhanced service will drive tips and other rewards (discussed further in Chapter 12).

long-term

Long-term, it will build guest frequency, providing more hours for employees and more tables to serve.

But how does the new way get implemented?

Typical Implementation

- Manager schedules a mandatory meeting.
- Manager delivers a long monologue on delivering better service.
- Employees nod their heads in agreement.
- Lots of short-term rah-rah that wears off faster than a sugar-rush.
- Nothing changes.
- Manager gives up (stupid book — doesn't work in the real world!).

Service That Sells! Implementation

- Manager solicits input from employees: What are we doing well? What needs to improve? How can better service be provided? Here are a few ideas we are considering, what do you think about them? What makes the job more difficult? What are guests saying? What prevents this from being a reality?
- Manager selects two to three employees to test the new procedures, including greetings, identifying why guests are visiting, situational selling, and so on.
- Manager schedules a *Fun-draising Rally*: "Learn how to make more money, get more hours and take care of more happy guests." (The very language used in the announcement is put into employee-benefiting terms.)
- At the rally, the manager introduces actual guests who describe how much they appreciate the new level of service. They tip more and visit more frequently.
- Employees who were the "test" describe how simple the new way is to do and how much better the service is.
- Manager introduces the first few components to focus on (identifying regulars as opposed to first-timers) and begins the process.
- Skeptical employees give it a try. Low and behold, it works (or they work elsewhere)!
- Managers continue to talk about it daily and gradually add more items into the mix.

Now That's Service That Sells!

The focus group is critical. It shows that managers are listening, willing to hear input, and ready to address obstacles that surface during the testing phase of implementation. This test involves a small group of employees, who, in turn, contribute suggestions to enhance the process. Once actual implementation begins, other employees see "their own people" are proponents and it's not another program driven from the top down.

> **As legendary baseball manager Casey Stengel said, "Managing is getting paid for home runs somebody else hits."**

Value the input you receive along the way. Respond accordingly, make enhancements as necessary, and propose solutions — don't just point out problems. As legendary baseball manager Casey Stengel said, "Managing is getting paid for home runs somebody else hits."

Approach the job as any sports team or professional band does: Conduct a "draft" or "tryouts" (to find talent), practice all the plays or music (training), cut the people who cannot perform (or re-direct them to new positions or employment), then play.

In the back of the house, managers oversee production. It's pretty black and white: What are the cook times? Are the recipes and portions followed? Is the plate to standard? Are proper sanitation and safety procedures followed?

Managing service, however, is a little more subjective. Out front, you have to manage processes and perceptions, which differ among guests. Difficult, yes. Impossible, hardly!

Coaching *Service That Sells!* can be easy. Choosing not to coach it is also easy. It's your choice. But you'll produce the best results when the employee behaviors you're after are repeated time after time. So coach the team daily, especially during the uncomfortable period of new-training implementation. The reward is worth it!

photocopying is prohibited

chapter nine

Be flexible, too. Providing outstanding service and hospitality is like a playground at recess. It may seem like chaos, but, in reality, teachers have established the parameters — no pushing, don't go past the edge of the playground, etc. The kids have flexibility and, more important, *fun* within those confines.

Instead of mandating a set way to do every single thing (i.e. you must greet every guest exactly like this, 'welcome to , I'll be your server today') in your restaurant, set ground rules as well as non-negotiable items (i.e the guest must be greeted before the door shuts), then allow employees to use their own style within those confines. You'll quickly see your top performers emerge, the ones who other employees look up to and want to work with.

Whatever you do, don't resort to nagging about every minute detail on how service is being delivered. If they are within the parameters, let them add their own personality. Otherwise, you'll end up creating mindless robots and take the fun out of the environment for the employees and the guests.

The non-negotiable items are service standards. For example: Greet guests within 45 seconds and inform them of the daily special and your favorite item. These rules cannot be broken, but you can still allow flexibility by not specifying exactly what must be said to guests. In turn, this opens the door for situational selling to occur.

When you impose too many standards, employees get bored, guests feel processed and service suffers.

When you impose too many standards, employees get bored, guests feel processed and service suffers. Don't lower standards, but do focus on what really matters to guests (eliminate those

that don't matter or allow flexibility about how it gets completed). If guests don't care, don't worry about how it is specifically done. If they do care, get on it!

This is your environment. Make the most of it. The old saying — "Expectations determine results" — is true. If managers send out the message that the restaurant won't be busy or a new menu item won't sell, they'll be right. Failure is addictive. Managers who walk into the restaurant dragging their butt and lacking enthusiasm will soon have a whole staff treating guests the same say. On the other hand, if managers believe the staff can set sales, profit or service records, they'll reach loftier heights than managers who have low expectations. Success is also addictive — pass it on!

Before and during the shift, challenge your employees to set goals and track their performance. The best managers keep score, putting systems in place to show everyone where they stand. Examples: Run tracking reports or product-mix reports, then post them on the expo line or near the POS terminal. In the back of the house, use timers to track cook times, then attach a score sheet or food cost reports to the time card or pay stub.

> **If managers send out the message that the restaurant won't be busy or a new menu item won't sell, they'll be right.**

Employees may believe they're doing an outstanding job until they see how others are performing. This brand of coaching or mentorship ensures that employees are accountable to someone in addition to themselves. That's why people who work out with personal trainers or a friend achieve better results — they don't want to let the other person down. Reward progress and improvement.

Managers have the ability to walk right into the middle of the action, seeing and hearing what's happening and making necessary adjustments. But if they're so focused on a single task at hand (comping a complaint, for instance), they'll end up missing everything going on around them, compromising their ability to coach performances.

Another shortcoming tends to occur when employees fall short of standards or expectations.

Typical managers do one of two things:

1 Ignore it and thus communicate to everyone else that it's OK.

2 Drop the hammer on the person.

If managers dwell on the negative, employees will start believing what they're hearing and eventually create their own demise. An abundance of positive feedback, on the other hand, will swing the pendulum in the other direction, and performances will get better.

To gauge how staff perceives management, walk through the kitchen, look at an item and ask: "Who made this?" If employees look the other way or ask "What's wrong?" or point the finger at someone else, they're expecting something negative to come out of your mouth. Follow up with: "This is what I'm talking about! Everyone take a look at this dish — all our dishes should look this good."

On occasions when you do need to take corrective action, order an "AND Sandwich." In other words, try to wrap two positives around the item to be corrected, and make sure you use the word "and" instead of "but."

Also try to avoid using "you." Employees tend to take it as a personal attack on them and lose sight of the behavior needing to be changed. That method is like getting pulled over by the police. The driver broke a law, but is mad at the officer (when in reality, it's the driver who made the mistake).

Typical Manager Feedback

- "Who made this — it looks terrible."
- "Sara, your station is filthy."
- "Get those drinks refilled."
- "What's your problem tonight?"
- "Smile, dammit!"
- "What did you do wrong now?"

Service That Sells! **Feedback**

- "Outstanding uniform — and it'll be even more impressive if you arrive at your scheduled time. Is there anything I can do to help?"
- "Great job suggesting the draft beer selection and you'll make even more money when you let the guests know it's only $1 more for the large!"
- "How can I help get the product to look like the last one?"
- "Great job explaining the specials to the last party, and if there's anything I can do to help ensure we seat the guests more quickly, let me know."

Now That's Service That Sells!

Take notice of how the previous feedback focused on "What can I do to help?" versus "What you did wrong." It's all about improving performance without sacrificing the respect of your employees. But if someone cannot or will not change, it's time to bring in qualified replacements.

A large casual-dining chain discovered that it actually makes money when it loses employees considered to be "anchors" dragging down the team. Turnover where you make money? It's true. How many guests did they not serve or seat properly? How much less productivity did the company receive from them?

Employees who don't have the talent or desire to deliver *Service That Sells!* need to be given a fair shot to work in a place where service of this caliber isn't expected. Hopefully, at a competing restaurant. They'll fit right in.

When implementing the new service strategy, some employees will have no problem whatsoever adapting (the 'superstar'). **A larger percentage will perform inconsistently but have the potential to become stars (the 'B' player).** A few others may simply refuse to do a thing you ask. Don't get too caught up trying to whip the minority into shape.

chapter nine

We've all heard of the 80/20 rule: Your superstars generate the most sales and profits. Not quite sure if it's so dramatic in the restaurant industry, but the key is the "B" player. This group typically makes up about 50 percent of your staff. To run your restaurant successfully, you need to have the B players improving their performance. They can do the job, but don't always seem to perform at a high enough level.

Each day they arrive, they ask: "Who's closing tonight?" If a manager who expects little is on duty, this group gives little. If the manager on duty is one who has high standards, demands plenty but rewards and recognizes, these employees perform at the higher level. Ultimately, it's the guests who benefit. Incentivize the 'B' player and you'll have 75 - 80 percent of your employees doing exactly what you want — delivering outstanding service. The others? Time to go elsewhere!

> **We've all heard of the 80/20 rule: Your superstars generate the most sales and profits.**

To get maximum impact in your operation, rank employees — one, two, three, etc. — in each key position. **On busy shifts, align the top talent with the top stations and the lower talent with the lower stations,** in the order of the rankings. It's much like an orchestra. If the first-chair performer isn't available, put in the second chair, not the fourth. The job simply becomes conducting the performance, knowing full well that one sour note could lead to ruin or "just another concert" for guests.

Servers are happiest when they make the most money. The restaurant is busy, service soars and tips flow like wine. **Set the energy level high and maintain it** — be a thermostat. Keep standards high and demand excellence. In return, reward performance, appreciate efforts to change and improve, and more will follow. After all, employees demand excellence in the person who controls the action and sets the tone — the manager!

chapter ten

CHAPTER 10

Coaching on Game Day

> Work on the business, not just in the business.

It's action-packed two or three shifts per day depending on hours of operation. There's a tendency for managers to roll up their sleeves to get through the day. After all, managers set the pace. How upbeat is the shift going to be today? What's today's focus?

As a manager, it's important to see things from an "aerial view." What's the big picture? How can the team get there? Where are we today? What needs to change to make tomorrow's shift better? How can time be spent to make guests' experiences really sizzle? Work on the business, not just in it.

As the assessment takes place, prioritize what needs to be done, working backward from the "perfect visit" to reach goals as quickly as possible. Implement and engrain behaviors on the two or three key items that will make the biggest impact on guests. Then focus on the next three and so on.

Evaluate the restaurant, employees and guests. What should guests' experiences look like? What is a perfect visit? Do employees know what it looks like? Start high — with the management team. Does each manager set the example? Model the behaviors?

> **How can time be spent to make guests' experiences really sizzle? Work on the business, not just in it.**

chapter ten

To close the gap and move toward service excellence, enlist the help of the staff to envision and write down what constitutes the perfect visit. Start outside the restaurant and describe what guests should see, feel and experience at each sizzle point. Post it for employees to see, highlighting each position's piece of the puzzle.

Run your shifts along the same route guests take, staying one step ahead of the action at all times. Address anything not up to the standard of the perfect visit.

Many restaurant companies initiate "walking paths" or "loops" to check on business. But if managers focus so intently on the step they're supposed to be doing, they'll tune out all other things going on around them.

In those instances, guests become invisible. And, pretty soon, the whole staff will follow suit, oblivious to guest's needs — the glass of clanking ice in need of more water or the check presenter, waved in the air, begging unanswered for reconciliation. It all becomes part of the scenery.

Great managers take "shift vital signs" as they work the room. Others simply walk the path because it's scheduled at a certain time of day. Like any other process or tool, it's only as effective as the person conducting the check.

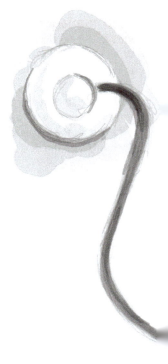

Typical Pulse Check

- Start at the front door and look around.
- Walk through the dining room.
- Visit three tables, because you have to: "Hi, I'm Joe, I'm the manager, how is everything?" By the time Joe makes it to the third table, the guests respond: "I know, you're Joe the manager — everything is OK."
- Go into the kitchen. Everything *looks* fine (from a distance).
- Grab a cup of coffee and feel good that nobody complained: "I run a great shift!"

What did the check miss? Drink refills, poor management of the wait, tables not maintained, dirty restrooms, bartender needs change, cook times more than 20 minutes, three guests wanting to pay but ignored as you walked by. At least you did the loop.

Watch out, however. Employees are a product of their environment. They'll mimic the behaviors they see on the floor. If managers slip on sizzle, so will the staff.

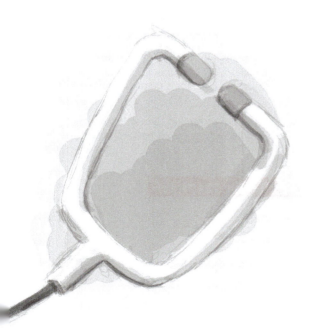

chapter ten

Service That Sells! Pulse Check

- Walk outside to check the micro-trash, front doors and entry and, in the process, thank any departing guests and welcome those arriving. As you move inside, you:

- Listen as the host greets arriving guests and thanks departing ones.

- Find out what the wait time is, head up to the bar, take a drink order while observing the bartender and thank a group for waiting: "It will be worth the wait!"

- As you move into the dining room, listen as the host seats a party, and provide immediate feedback for a job well done.

- Look over the kitchen tickets or whiteboard for indications of first-time guests. Introduce yourself to those guests and welcome them to the restaurant.

- Pick up the tea pitcher and refill a few glasses as you check on tables.

- Having noticed the tables need pre-bussing, flag down the server and service assistant to get them on top of it immediately. (Feedback: "Great job selling dessert and it'll be easier for the guests to enjoy it if we remove the entrée dishes.")

- A quick detour to the restroom to ensure it's spotless (sending a service assistant to check on the restroom of the opposite sex).

- Then it's on to the kitchen (yes, you washed your hands!).

- What's selling? How are cook times? Touch the dishes — do they look like they could be in a TV commercial? Any bottlenecks? Running low on any product or prep? A few pats on the back for a great shift and it's time to check sales.

- Run a sales report. Are you ahead of projection? Slow? Do you need to cut labor or get the servers to suggestively sell even better to meet the day's goal?

Now That's Service That Sells!

(H.O.M.E.S.)
Hands-On Management Ensures Success

In the previous examples of the Typical Pulse Check versus the *Service That Sells!* Pulse Check, both managers followed a similar path yet produced dramatically different results. Typical managers merely go through the motions, not paying enough attention to their surroundings. Astute managers have keen restaurant senses, hearing buzzers going off, sensing empty ice machines, seeing things no ordinary human can. They uncover and fix problems before guests become aware that anything was even wrong.

Break down your own loop, adding an action step at every stop. Examples:

- "Check the front door" becomes "Open the door and welcome guests."
- "Check the host stand" becomes "Welcome a party of guests and seat them."
- "Check the dining room" becomes "Visit first-time guests and introduce a new employee to a regular guest."

Focus on four to five quick-hit items to look for while going through the action steps previously described. Your process of checking needs to be hands-on, not just visual. Can you really tell if some things are done properly without up-close inspection? A sticky table, after all, looks fine from a distance (but not to the guest sitting there).

chapter ten

1 Open the door and welcome arriving guests/thank departing guests.
- Micro-trash check (out to first row of cars).
- Glass and brass clean?
- Floors clean and dry?
- Great first impressions for arriving guests?

2 Welcome a party at the host stand.
- How long is the wait?
- Hosts properly welcoming all guests?
- Menus to waiting guests (activities for kids)?
- Host stand stocked with all supplies (clean menus, kid's menus, crayons, pens, pagers)?
- Recognize a host for something outstanding.

3 Seat a party.
- Listen to hosts describing specials, identifying why guests are visiting.
- Any needs at tables you walk by as you seat?
- Was the guest quoted an accurate wait time?
- Why is the guest visiting today?
- Tables need to be cleared? Drink refills? Table maintenance?

4 Make a drink at the bar.
- Bartender keeping up?
- Servers suggesting drink specials, wines or premium liquors (look at tickets)?
- Bar NCO (neat, clean, organized)?
- All supplies stocked? Change needed?
- Liquor run needed for back stock?
- Recognize the bartender for job well done.

5 Check the restroom (and send someone of the opposite sex to the other one).
- Floors clean, debris-free and dry?
- Mirrors and sinks clean and dry?
- Toilet paper/paper towels stocked?
- Restroom checks being done by staff?
- Check stalls and/or urinals.
- Wash hands.

6 Deliver food to a table (look around at other tables!).
- Cook times to standard?
- Plate presentations top-notch?
- Listen to other servers as you deliver food.
- Refills needed, tables clean, checks tendered quickly?
- Servers having fun and interacting with guests?

7 Check on a guest.
- Food outstanding?
- Why are they visiting?
- Get their names. ("My name is , and you are?")
- Invite them back.
- Deliver a free dessert sample or appetizer sample to an unsuspecting guest.
- Recognize a server and pass on compliments.

8 Make a dish in the kitchen.
- Cook times to standard?
- Prep levels maintained?
- Quality and plate presentation top-notch?
- Stations clean and organized, sanitation standards met?
- Take a food temperature (check a different product each hour).
- Recognize a kitchen team member for something great you just saw.

chapter ten

9 Prepare a carryout order.
- Phone — *selling* or taking an order?
- Order times quoted accurately?
- Listen to phone greetings, suggestive selling, quoting accurate times, repeating, thanking.
- Double-check order accuracy.
- Thank staff for being productive, fun and upbeat.

10 Run sales and product mix reports.
- Sales meeting projection?
- Product mix — modify any prep items as needed.
- Communicate with the team — sales needs, running low on items, suggest a specific item, thank staff for exceeding goals.
- Make necessary labor adjustments.

11 Recognize an employee — one per hour (minimum).
- 30-second review: What is working? What is making their job difficult? How can I help?
- Praise something done right.

Now That's SERVICE THAT SELLS!

At one point or another, virtually every manager has tried to run a restaurant by him or herself. Can't be done, can it? You end up missing things, even running the pulse check every hour.

Teach employees and other managers to think. Teach them to see what you see. Teach them to look for what you're looking for. If there are items below standard, deliver feedback that teaches employees or managers to think and act. The more the employees see and do, the more time you can spend talking to guests and hearing how well you are doing!

Typical Manager

- "How come you haven't maintained those tables?"
- "How come those guests don't have drink refills?"
- Nag, nag, nag.

Service That Sells! Manager

- "Let's go through the five key points in your area — what do you see we're doing right?" (Deliver appropriate praise.)
- "Now, what needs attention?"
- If employees don't see the things you're looking for, give clues.
- Offer solutions or assistance. Ask what they can do differently next time to avoid those situations.

Now That's Service That Sells!

Encourage employees to do a mini-pulse check in their area

along with some common areas and, pretty soon, they'll be truly zeroing in on what delights guests. Develop a list of responsibilities for everyone — no matter what section they're in, what position they hold or who they are.

chapter ten

> # "Some areas to consider "everyone's responsibility:"

The front door.
Anyone near the door needs to welcome incoming guests. If the staff member can't perform the seating, he or she can still say: "The host will be right with you." Eye contact and a smile also help set a positive, comforting tone. As guests leave, anyone can open the door, thank them and invite them back.

The Hospitality Zone.
Employees make eye contact with any guest who approaches within 3-4 steps and verbally acknowledges any guest who gets within 1-2 steps. In the dining room, staff, including service assistants, can say "hello" and "welcome" to the newly arrived. If employees aren't interacting with guests, a few sizzle points just fizzled. Staff should also take notice of puzzled or frustrated looks — guests waiting to be greeted, place an order, pay the check, etc. Take care of their needs or get someone who can!

Restrooms.
Yes, someone is ultimately responsible for them, but if an employee is in there, he or she can pick up the paper towels on the floor, flush the toilets and urinals, and wipe down the sinks (don't forget to wash your hands once you are finished). Guests don't deserve to walk into a filthy restroom.

Refills.
Servers, when refilling beverages in their own section, can also look around for other opportunities to top off water and/or tea glasses. Hosts can also assist when they are caught up on seating guests.

Table maintenance.
Whenever there are unwanted plates and glasses on a table — whether it's an assigned section or not — service staff can remove them.

Food delivery.
Food doesn't taste great if it sits under a heat lamp. Get the food to the table!

Guests deserve personal attention from every employee. After all, they're doing the restaurant a favor by dining there. When the entire team pitches in, it shows guests that they're the top priority.

 Appendix D contains a small card (also available as a downloadable file at www.pencominternational.com) to carry around and use when doing pulse checks in your restaurant. Stop, look, listen and coach — make it an hourly routine as you work the room. When you're alert, there are many things you'll see and be able to improve — sales and service levels chief among them. Most importantly, the guests will be leaving saying, "*Now That's Service That Sells!*"

chapter eleven

CHAPTER 11

Reinforcing the Message

> It's 11 a.m. (or 5 p.m.) — do you know how your guests are being cared for?

Somewhere between initial training and today, a percentage of employees' knowledge and skill is lost. How much or how little depends on the frequency of practice and reinforcement. Guests, meanwhile, don't care about the past. They're interested in the service they're receiving at the present time. Are you confident your employees can deliver?

Try a little word association, having staff members write down three things that pop into their minds when they hear each of the following terms. *Don't spell the words, only say them.* Once employees are done, they should compare lists with a partner to observe the number of matches. See Appendix E for common words associated with these terms.

Run _____

Sell _____

Sale _____

Buy _____

Strike _____

Fall _____

Set _____

Fair _____

Out of the 24 possible answers, chances are most people matched fewer than six (25%). This list has eight well-known words, but, by not spelling them out, employees may hear something different than intended ("cell" versus "sell," for instance). In addition, many of these words have multiple meanings. "Set" has more than 460 and "run" more than 390!

Why conduct this exercise? People often assume everyone is thinking or interpreting words the same way. Managers ask servers to suggestively sell. What does that mean? A few of their sales lines may be:

- "You don't want anything else, do you?"
- "Anything else?"
- "If I don't ask, we lose points on the mystery shop."

These are all examples (albeit weak ones) of suggestive selling and undoubtedly have been heard at one time or another, maybe in your own restaurant. Telling a host to "greet the guest" could be interpreted as:

- "Two?"
- "Four for dinner?"
- "Just one?"
- "Smoking or non?"
- "Carryout or do you need a table?"

Again, all of these examples fit the definition of 'greet', but they don't sizzle. It's like asking kids if they cleaned their rooms. Is their definition of "clean" the same as the parent's?

By the end of this book, you may know how to deliver *Service That Sells!* But ask yourself: Are employees on the same wavelength? The more you talk about service, the more focused and adept you'll become at raising the bar of excellence for your guests. Ideas are the easy part, daily execution by every employee will make the difference!

Here are a few easy-to-implement tools and tips to ensure employees get their daily dose of *Service That Sells!*

Pre-Shift Meeting.

Also known as the huddle, Alley Rally and other things, the pre-shift meeting is nothing new, but is it even being done in your operation? Do you conduct one at least 75 percent of the shifts? Is it effective? Is it done properly? Is your definition of a pre-shift meeting:

Typical Pre-Shift Meeting

- One sided monologue led by the managers.
- Manager drones on about useless information or harp on things going wrong, sucking the energy out of employees.
- Managers ask questions that yield little, so they can check off the "conduct pre-shift meeting" box on their daily checklist. For example, "Do you know the special today?" "Can you suggestively sell dessert?" "Does everyone know how to upsell from well to call brands?"
- Employees nod their head "yes" each time managers ask a question such as the ones above.
- Nothing changes (including the downward sales spiral).

Service That Sells! Pre-Shift Meeting

- Two-way dialogue between managers and employees.
- Manager asks questions, but with different results:
- "John, describe the special for everyone."
- "Susie, top John's description of the special."
- "Matthew, how many are you going to sell tonight? How much is the special?"
- "Courtney, I order a vodka tonic, what would your response be?"
- "Leticia, I order a draft beer, what would you say?"
- "Todd, what would you recommend for dessert?"
- "Jane, I arrive at the host desk and have never been here before. Tell me what you are going to say as you escort me to the table."
- Manager reviews a recipe of the day and allows everyone to have a small taste.
- Employees are asked to set personal goals for the shift (check average, number of guest names, sales of specific items, etc.).
- The guest experience, sales and tips ROCK!

Now That's Service That Sells!

chapter eleven

The little voice inside you may be saying: "But in my store, we can't do a pre-shift meeting all at one time and get everyone together."

There are two options:

1 Don't conduct the pre-shift meeting (like many of your competitors) and hope everything goes well.

2 Figure out a way to review the key items just mentioned.

It's easiest to conduct the meetings at one time (keep them very short), but if scheduling requires flexibility, schedule them at 30-minute intervals (5:00, 5:30 and 6:00).

Remember T.O.D. — training on demand

What does the staff need to know today to be successful and sizzle the guests? The goal is to focus on the business — hearing compliments from guests, observing the team in action, praising and re-directing versus working in a station and putting out fires.

If the interval system won't work, spend a short time with each employee as he or she arrives. As you go over the information in the style previously described, take the opportunity to review appearance standards and deliver praise whenever possible. A leading fast-casual chain calls it TIP/TOP.

Now That's **SERVICE THAT SELLS!**

TIP — Talk Into Position.

Spend 30-60 seconds role-playing the items on page 119 with one or a small group of employees. Ask questions so the employees are reciting the information versus the manager. Provide praise and suggestions as necessary. Set goals with the employees to ensure they maximize their potential. Thirty seconds apiece for 20 employees — that's 600 seconds or 10 minutes of a manager's time. It's a great way to set the tone and pace of the shift.

TOP — Talk Out of Position.

Spend 30 seconds as employees are getting ready to leave. Review your observations, sales numbers or other relevant information. What worked well tonight? What opportunity is there to improve next shift? What was the best guest compliment you heard? Any guest suggestions? Did employees hit their sales goals discussed during the TIP? Provide plenty of feedback and recognition. Why would any of the employees want to find a new job if they receive a mini-appraisal and an opportunity to provide input each and every day? *Now That's* Service That Sells!

Still worried your pre-shift meetings will be drab? Think back to your school days for a minute. Multiple-choice tests seemed easier than other forms of testing, didn't they? You could figure out an answer from the list of possibilities. But was the information really understood? To succeed at fill-in-the-blank tests, on the other hand, you really had to know your stuff.

Lead your pre-shift meetings with a fill-in-the-blank approach.

It's far more effective in helping employees retain information. Also be sure to infuse daily variety and change. Otherwise, the meetings can stagnate and bore employees.

Other pre-shift meeting suggestions:

Use a whiteboard.

> Communicate daily specials, featured items, focus of the day, etc., so employees can review it prior to hitting the floor.

Provide 3x5 shift cards.

> As employees arrive, they receive a card filled out by the manager on duty. It describes special assignments for the day, featured items or specials, desired food and beverage descriptions — all to be used as reference throughout the shift.

Recipe of the day.

> Select an item or three to review with the front-of-the-house staff. In the back of the house, have kitchen staff prepare the item exactly to standard. Cooks get to hone their preparation skills, servers get to taste items which, in turn, they can describe to guests in better detail: "The chef prepared one for the staff earlier today and it's outstanding!" Who can resist? One item per day and the menu will be completely trained in one or two months in a typical restaurant.

Around the dial.

> One by one, have front-of-the-house staff name a characteristic, price, wine suggestion or other information about a featured menu item. What's missing? Who provided the best descriptions? Managers don't have all the information — employees do. This exercise encourages employees to share best practices and allows employees to hear from their peers, not the boss.

Trainer for a day.

Assign a menu-item training for the day and let an employee lead that part of the pre-shift meeting. He or she will learn how to prepare a training message, ask effective questions, praise and re-direct, etc. With the manager nearby to provide assistance, employees can become more comfortable presenting in front of a group and may even lay the groundwork to become actual trainers down the road.

> **When people teach, they learn. Did you notice a great host greeting or server suggestion? Share these best practices at the next meeting.**

Reality TV.

Assign a menu item or portion of the menu to small groups of employees. Have them prepare a short video or presentation for the next shift meeting. A twist on the old class favorite Show and Tell. When people teach, they learn. Did you notice a great host greeting or server suggestion? Share these best practices at the next meeting. Videotape it so others not on duty can receive the benefit of seeing excellence in action.

Health kick.

Ask for volunteers to suggest modifications to the existing menu to suit the latest diet trends: "What items do we serve that are low-carb?" "How can we make item X into a low-carb or vegetarian option?" Additionally, review food allergies so employees are aware of items containing MSG, peanuts, and so on. Do employees know some items are prepared in a beef or chicken stock so even if there seems to be no meat, it really isn't vegetarian?

Description prescription.

A great way to jazz up pre-shift meetings is to have employees come up with unique descriptive words or phrases for their favorite menu items. Throw out a question to get it rolling and see who can come up with the most descriptive phrases. Post them in the break area or communication board so others can use the ideas.

Quote of the day.

Post a quote about service, motivation or positive news each day. Employees are barraged with nothing but negative information in the papers and on TV. Post some good news or a funny quote to disconnect them from the negativity and put them into the proper frame of mind. Control the atmosphere (you are the thermostat) — success is contagious — pass it on!

Do I know you?

Have employees write down one interesting fact about themselves, then list the facts on duplicated Bingo-style game boards and pass them out. During lulls in the shift, employees need to find out which person each of the facts describes. Once they complete the card, they win a prize. It's an effective way to promote teamwork and get to know each other.

Useless information challenge.

Each day select four to five different items for servers or hosts to uncover about guests. Not only will it add variety to the shift and the experience, it creates fun interaction with the guests (far different from the competition). For example:

- Guest who drove the farthest distance to get here.
- Guest who drove the shortest distance.
- Guest celebrating the most senior birthday.
- Family with the most children.

Power cards.

Create a series of cards — bound or kept in a small binder — that contain all the relevant information for menu items, or have descriptions and ingredients of popular drinks. Employees can quiz each other (or the manager can lead quizzes) throughout the shift during slow times. For servers and hosts, recommended add-ons or wines to suggest with the item will reinforce the behaviors. For back-of-the-house employees, use the cards to review recipes and plate-presentation standards.

Guest trivia.

> Have servers or hosts ask guests (especially kids) a trivia question for the chance to win a discount or free item. Use questions from board games or have your own ("What is today's special?"). Hosts can ask the question as they escort guests to their table. Servers can encourage a mini-competition among the tables in their section and reward a prize to the winner.

The restaurant landscape is filled with competitors who deliver ordinary experiences extraordinarily well. Shake things up. Try something new. Be different every day. Your delivery of interactive service will wow guests, sending them out the door wondering how great their next visit will be...and it will be soon!

Training on demand, meanwhile, will keep employees on their toes, reinforcing communication, knowledge and service skills. It also fosters fun interaction with guests. And fun translates into great experiences. Look in the mirror. YOU run the shift. The experience of the guest is a reflection of you. Not the GM or owner, you, the M.O.D. (manager on duty). Will your guests leave saying, *Now That's Service That Sells!?*

chapter twelve

CHAPTER 12

Rallying the Troops

> If you want to enhance the guest experience, you have to improve the employee experience.
> — TJ Schier

To truly deliver outstanding service to every guest, every visit, the whole staff needs to be trained and ready to deliver. Employees are leery of managers who tell their employees "be nicer," "provide better service" and "work harder." All the while, the managers are treating them like mushrooms (keeping them in the dark and feeding them manure).

To maximize the effectiveness of change, demonstrate to employees how they'll benefit from the new service focus and treat them better. The number one motivating factor for employees is full appreciation of their efforts. If they currently give 95 percent and receive no positive feedback, why should they give 100 percent?

Incentives focus on two groups: the A players (who already deliver great service) and the B players (who have the ability but use it selectively). Incentives, contests and recognition help ensure the A players are motivated to continue doing what they do best and to get better at it. Unfortunately, they represent a small percentage of the employee base. The majority — the B players — is wondering: "Who's closing tonight?"

Of the two groups, B is the most important to the success of your restaurant. To perform at a high level, B players need someone or a system to hold them accountable. If nobody's keeping an eye on them or expecting great performance, they can slack with the best of them. Incentives, contests and recognition drive this group onward and upward.

> **Employees are leery of managers who tell their employees "be nicer," "provide better service" and "work harder."**

chapter twelve

Not all incentives, contests and recognition, however, are created equal. **Which would be more effective incentive program for a health club?**

Work out 100 times in six months and receive a chance to win a cruise.

Or:

Work out 25 times — get a free T-shirt, 50 times — a free month's dues, 100 times — a $50 gift card.

Members could work out 100 times in the first example and still lose. They're in shape, which means they performed their end of the deal, but likely received zero incentive in return. In fact, many would have probably given up once they realized they had little chance of winning. In the second example, meanwhile, members scored numerous prizes.

The key to long-term success is setting intermediate benchmarks. Like the football team who gains 10 yards in four plays to keep going, incentives allow employees to celebrate small successes as they march on to larger ones. How the employees are treated through this process will determine their ability to stick with it. Managers are training partners, ensuring that employees show up every day for their workouts. Managers encourage, challenge and reward. But do managers know how?

> **The key to long-term success is setting intermediate benchmarks.**

A word on incentives: Don't confuse them with a lottery. "Sell an item and be in the drawing for a trip" is not effective. Many people sell and someone is lucky enough to win. There is no correlation between the performance (how much someone sold) and winning.

Incentives are ideal to drive changes in behavior. Having a grand prize is great — it has sex appeal and keeps people motivated. However, there needs to be rewards for any employee who increases sales or performance levels. If not, he or she will do additional work and won't be rewarded for it.

Employee recognition isn't a program. It should be an integral part of the culture, where incentives and contests are tools used to mold behaviors and move the team to a higher level. Here are a number of ideas to help get the ball rolling:

chapter twelve

incentives & contests

FUN-D RAISER.

Servers or bartenders receive one point for every $1 in incremental sales they drive. First, determine and communicate the benchmark check average in your operation. If, at the end of the shift, an employee has served 100 guests with a check average a dollar higher than the benchmark, he or she would earn 100 points for the $100 in incremental sales generated. Points are saved up for prizes.

This contest also works well for selling specific items or lowering food costs. The key to success is utilizing the current benchmark (or historical average) and only rewarding performance exceeding it. The contest becomes self-funding because money is only paid out (in the form of prizes) when additional sales are generated (or costs lowered).

Keep in mind that this contest can work for selling specific items, but past experience has proven that selling more of one appetizer usually cannibalizes another so the net effect is zero. Allowing employees to focus on check average gives them the flexibility to use situational selling, as discussed earlier.

SERVER BOUNCE-BACK COUPONS.

Servers provide each table with a bounce-back coupon (with a short expiration date) at the end of the meal. It can be as simple as a package deal or as elaborate as a scratch-off mystery discount. Servers write their names on the coupons and whoever gets the most redeemed during the contest period wins the grand prize. Others receive points or prizes at various levels. Not surprising, you'll find a direct correlation between the service guests are receiving and the number of coupons redeemed.

NAME GAME.

Employees earn pins or prizes for learning a pre-set number of guests' names. This simple contest encourages interaction and underscores who pays the bills. A leading buffet chain rewards employees who learn 100 names. Ask employees to focus on getting and using guests' names during their visits. Everyone appreciates being called by name versus being treated like a number.

"GET TO KNOW ME" BINGO.

To encourage servers and hosts to interact with guests, create a bingo card containing various items for employees to uncover while running their shift. Examples could include: Guest who plays tennis, guest who has more than two children, guest who works within two miles of the restaurant and so on. Employees will have to use their imagination and skills to discover the information. As they talk to guests, they "get the square" when they find a guest with the item they're looking for. Prizes are awarded for first bingo, completing all squares, etc.

CLOSEST TO THE PIN.

Have servers try to predict how many of a specific item they'll sell for the day. In the back of the house, kitchen staff can try to guess total food waste, number of remakes, busiest product hour or ideal food cost versus theoretical. A word of advice: Do a "farthest from the pin" (person who exceeds projection by the most) so employees don't sell a certain number and then stop selling to win the contest.

COOK TIME/QUALITY.

Have a specified number of points, lottery tickets or tickets for a drawing available to the kitchen staff for the shift. Every time a product goes over the specified time or doesn't meet standards, points are deducted or tickets are lost. Staff divides up whatever remains at the end. Peer pressure is more effective than management pressure and it promotes teamwork and quality.

FIND THE DOT, CLEAN THE SPOT.

Place date labels around those hard-to-clean places, including under the dish machine, behind equipment, under stacks of cups or boxes, etc. Basically, any place you need to clean. Employees find the dots, clean the spots and earn points and/or prizes.

WORLD RECORDS.

Create a series of records to encourage productivity and competition. Simple tasks such as fastest production or prep times, safety records, test completion times, drink mixing, side duties completed and so on can make work fun.

What prizes should you hand out? Which are the best and most effective? Don't assume you know. Ask! Find out what makes employees tick. Learning what they do in their spare time will shed light on what rewards are ideal.

chapter twelve

 There are two great books to help you out: "Playing Games at Work: 52 Best Incentives, Contests and Rewards for the Hospitality Industry" and "Service That Sells!" — *visit www.pencominternational.com to order.*

Cut the custom deal. Employees want the best station? Fine, they need to run the highest check average. They want to be off early on Friday nights? Fine, they need to do certain side work. If they don't live up to their end of the bargain, the deal is off. Just don't forget to live up to your end.

Is it harder to manage this way? Seems like it, but it really isn't. The expectations are clearly set: perform a certain way and receive an agreed upon reward.

Many employees will see this as unfair. Unfair? Unfair is paying employees the same wages for far different productivity levels. Unfair is giving a 5 percent raise to the great employee and 3 percent to the average employee. Unfair is keeping the slackers around who don't produce. Unfair is piling the extra work on the superstars.

Fair is rewarding and compensating employees for the productivity they provide.
Fair is having A players work the busy shifts, making the most of the opportunity. Reward your great performers. Get rid of your non-performers. That's fair!

Rewards don't have to be lavish. And how they're presented is as important as the reward itself. Insincere gifts from managers (or grumbling about how much prizes cost) won't mean as much or may even drive away employees quicker. Words of encouragement and praising are free and very meaningful. As the old saying goes: "Well-done should come out of a manager's mouth more often than just talking about steak temperature."

> **Employees want the best station? Fine, they need to run the highest check average.**

Cash tends to be a tempting incentive, but its effects wear off quickly. A 20-dollar bill for selling the most of an item will blend with the tips and get spent on bills, gas or food. There is no link between the performance and the reward. A $20 gift card presented in a company note card will drive home the connection. If cash is used, try $1 gold coins. Most employees will save them or at least remember where they came from if they get spent.

Cash is important to everyone. It's just not the most effective motivator. If it were, all servers would focus on increasing sales and check averages since they get a cut of the action in the form of tips. Many restaurants include the gratuity in the bill — at least for large parties. Is the service any better? Policies like these punish the good servers and reward the weak servers.

Remember, the key is to find out what excites employees and give it to them in the form of incentives. Employees, meanwhile, must get the job done in order to continue to receive the incentives. It's a performance agreement. If they fall short, the deal is off.

Here's how to appreciate your employees:

Thank them — verbally or with handwritten notes.

Listen to them — solicit input and suggestions. Reward cost-saving and sales-driving ideas.

+ Ask them to join an employee council to help recommend solutions to issues.
+ Award choice of station. They become King or Queen of the Hill and someone has to knock them down by outperforming them!
+ Allow them to write their own schedule for a week.
+ Provide additional development or training. Recognition separating employees from their peers is quite a motivator.
+ Need to cover hard-to-fill shifts or stations? Offer incentive pay — a dollar or two extra per hour. If employees don't want to train others because they'll lose tips, offer a trainer wage to encourage participation.

Other winning ideas:

- Paid time off.
- Free meals.
- A pass allowing employees' family to come in for a free meal. Don't forget to stop by and visit them.
- "Get out of work free" card (15/30/60 minutes).
- "Get out of *side work* free" card.
- Free haircut, car wash, oil change or dry cleaning.
- Gift cards for video game or movie rentals, gas, other restaurants, electronic stores, etc.
- Movie pass — combined with paid time off for a big wow.
- Lottery tickets — where else could employees have a chance to retire immediately?
- Calling card.
- Picture on a "wall of fame" or "world records" board. Track highest sales, check average, lowest cook times, fastest prep times, most positive compliments, etc. People will do extraordinary things to set a record.
- Logoed hats and key chains.
- Pins. They're conversation starters with guests and set people apart.
- A 10-cent raise (it costs only $4 per week if recipient works 40 hours).
- Name a day or part of the office or restaurant after them.

Also make it a point to catch employees doing the right things:

Showing up on time. "Thanks for coming in on time today. I wish all employees focused on punctuality like you."

Doing what they're supposed to do. "Great job portioning out the chicken."

Making improvements in areas they were weak in. "We talked last week about consistency and I wanted to thank you for the effort you have made in ensuring each dish looks exactly like the recipe."

Uniform compliance. "Great job on the uniform today. Hey, everyone, take a look at how Jeff is dressed today. This is how it's done!"

Positive guest comments. "Jenny, the guests at table 42 complimented how nice you were while seating them. I really appreciate the effort — it's helping build sales and it makes my job much easier. Thanks!"

Top performance on a busy shift. "Way to go kitchen team — record sales and no mistakes! Performance like this ensures our servers can focus on the guests. I really appreciate!"

Budgets achieved/costs lowered. "John, thanks for the extra attention on minimizing waste over the last week. Our food cost went down .1 percent. Keep it up!"

Profitable suggestive selling. "Awesome job, Sally, suggesting the premium liquors to table 27. I'd like to post the line you used with the guests in the break area if that's all right."

Product quality. "Who made this? Looks great! Let's see them all come out like this."

Production times. "Nice job in the kitchen with cook times — it's really helping us turn tables!"

Covering a shift or extra work. "I really appreciate you coming in early today to cover for the no-show. The guests are lucking out today getting you as a server."

Great ideas. "Great suggestion to eliminate the bottleneck at the expo line, Susie. Everyone will benefit."

Taking one for the team. "I know you didn't agree with the decision, but I really appreciate you supporting it during the shift."

chapter twelve

 A word of caution: Incentives can never get the wrong people to do the right things. If a sub-par employee is terminated who was working 40 hours per week at $8 per hour, the $320 can be used to provide raises — a 25-cent raise to 32 employees who work 40 hours per week. Or, better yet, a few large raises for great employees and moderate raises for those who are improving. The rest of the money can go toward rewards and incentive prizes.

You can't win every guest alone. Incentives, contests and rewards will help you get things done through your people. The restaurant wins when everyone works together toward common goals. The result? Sales, profits and retention levels rise while stress levels fall. *Now That's* Service That Sells!

chapter thirteen

CHAPTER 13

Marketing

Marketing was placed toward the end of this book for a reason — get everything else done first. Far too many companies spend millions of dollars marketing an inferior product and average service. But if you promote a dud, guess what? More people will know it's a dud.

A more cost-effective approach is to implement the action steps prescribed in the chapters of this book. If you do, you'll create a word-of-mouth buzz driving free P.R. and valuable referrals.

Once your restaurant is running at the desired levels of service, you can unleash the marketing beast. Until then, it makes no sense to attract more guests into a restaurant that doesn't sizzle. In fact, many marketing ideas — clever ones, too — have bitten the dust because the service supporting them was merely average or OK.

The best sequence? Fix the product, make it outstanding, then market it. You can call on numerous marketing strategies such as TV commercials, radio advertising, remotes, coupons in the local paper, newspaper advertising — even an "Under New Management" banner. These *external* methods, however, aren't nearly as important as what you do *internally* to get guests to come back.

> **But if you promote a dud, guess what? More people will know it's a dud.**

Take a moment to think about successful restaurants around your neighborhood. Which ones advertise? How do they do it? Many have built a very loyal guest base by providing tremendous service and by making everyone feel important — like they're family — like they're a name, not a number.

chapter thirteen

It's a fact:

Guests want to go where they're known. And the easiest way to know them is to ask for their name, remember it, and use it whenever they visit. If appropriate, purchase a point-and-shoot camera to record the fun times guests have in your operation. Hang the photographs in a public place, honoring your regulars and attracting the attention of your newcomers.

Do whatever it takes to make guests feel special. Take a sincere interest in their everyday lives, try to anticipate their needs, make them out to be the most important person in your store. After all, they're the reason you're in business. They'll also be extremely receptive to your external-marketing efforts, especially those designed to improve visit frequency.

Whatever time and money you decide to spend on these efforts, it's wise to invest an equal, if not greater amount, on ramping up your internal marketing — the quality of service your staff provides along with the marketing messages communicated to guests while they're in the house.

That's right — *in the house*. The mistake often made is to view a promotion as an end in itself. To be effective, however, you have to think beyond merely attracting guests in the door. You also have to encourage them to make purchases, enjoy the experience your employees provide and, most important, come back another day — all of which requires well-trained employees who can speak to the promotion and execute at the point of sale. Guests can't participate in the event if they don't know what's going on.

> **In planning a promotion, try to determine where you want to end up before you rush out of the gate.**

In planning a promotion, try to determine where you want to end up before you rush out of the gate. First, project the revenue you're likely to generate, then allocate a percentage of it to cover your costs — costs you've determined in advance. If you're after short-term success, be happy with nothing less than a 10-dollar return on every dollar invested.

If, for example, you've projected $5,000 in promotional revenue, the budget should be around $500 for the event itself. On the other hand, you could accept a four-to-one return if you can expect long-term benefits — primarily repeat business from guests participating in the event.

Too often restaurants are willing to pile up promotional costs on the front end with little or no idea if they'll turn a profit. Optimism is no substitute for intelligent planning.

chapter thirteen

backtime

Speaking of planning, the best course of action is to "backtime" the essentials of the promotion. Working in reverse, day by day, plan all of the steps needed to execute the event. You may discover that time constraints prohibit you from doing everything you originally wanted to do. The idea is to spot trouble before you've dug in your heels.

As you backtime each day of the promotion, detail only the task, the person responsible for completing the task and the time by which the task should be completed. It's a tough but rewarding job that forces you to think through each detail of what needs to be done.

incentives, contests and rewards

Don't forget about including incentives, contests and rewards, either. Used in concert with the promotion, they can fuel enthusiasm while keeping promotional elements top-of-mind with employees and guests alike.

Guarantee message.

It begins with a button or sticker on the employee or a table tent. Guests become managers — they watch employees' performance when the manager cannot. When visiting a convenience store with a sign above the register, "If you fail to get a receipt, your purchase is free," what is the customer thinking? "Please forget, please forget, please forget." The employee knows the customer is watching and provides the receipt. Of course, the real reason the sign is there is so the cashier enters the sales into the register, but those thoughts aren't going through the customers' minds — they want something free!

By using a guarantee message in the restaurant, managers can get what they want, whether it's suggestions, sales entered properly or hosts mentioning specials. Guests, meanwhile, have a little fun trying to catch employees making a mistake.

Some ideal guarantee messages could be:

If the server fails to suggest _____, the guest receives a free $5 gift card.

If the host doesn't mention the special, dessert is on us.

If the time at the drive-thru window is more than _____ seconds, the meal is free.

If the actual wait time versus the quoted wait time is more than 10 minutes off, receive a free appetizer for the table!

If the server fails to show the dessert tray, dessert is on us.

chapter thirteen

The beauty of this approach is that the system manages employees when nobody is around. Leverage the impact by training employees properly and make sure these types of suggestions aren't going on:

- "I have to suggest the appetizer platter tonight or you get it free, so would you like one?"
- "If I don't ask, I get in trouble, so would you like the special tonight?"
- "Here's the dessert tray. We have to show it. You don't want anything do you?"

Worse yet, poor employees might purposely not suggest the item so the restaurant has to provide it for free. Those employees need to work elsewhere! The chapter on "situational selling" provides many effective suggestions. Combining an incentive program with situational sales training and a guarantee message will ensure incredible results.

Other promotions.

After you've lassoed new business and simultaneously trained your staff to maximize its service and sales potential during the promotion, consider using bouncebacks to generate repeat traffic. Bouncebacks are promotional offerings that are good the *next* time guests come in. Make them compelling and create a sense of urgency to redeem by making them good for only a short time.

Here are a few other ideas to try once the restaurant is ready to be shown off:

Charity events.

Have an evening when a percentage of sales is donated to a local charity. Contact the press to cover the event. Guests will be encouraged to try the restaurant and public relations will help build word-of-mouth. You may even get an article in the paper from the reporter who experienced the new level of service.

VIG card.

To reward regulars and build loyalty, create a "very important guest" card. Whether it offers a progressive discount or a reward (spend $100 and receive a $10 gift certificate), guests will be more likely to return. The card also signals that the guest is a regular! If possible, use the POS system to track the promotion.

Loyalty programs tend to work better than discounts because guests feel more bonded to the brand and it doesn't cheapen the image of the restaurant like discounts tend to do. Airlines have perfected the system with their frequent fliers. Take a page from their book and modify it to work in your restaurant.

Fundraisers.

Invite schools or community groups in on various evenings and donate a part of the proceeds to their cause. Most restaurants need weekday business. Set up a system with the 20 or so schools around you and assign each a specific day of the month (Monday–Thursday over four weeks). Donate 5 percent of the sales. It's an effective way to stay involved in the community and encourage visits from guests who haven't come in for a while.

Sales bingo.

Provide guests with a punch card to try a variety of different items. Once a row on the card is completed, they receive a prize and recognition. Many restaurants have taken this approach with "beers of the world." You can also try it to encourage guests to order appetizers, desserts, a variety of specials, or a string of lunch visits during the business week.

Local offices and churches.

Have they sworn off the place because of inadequate service in the past? Send them an invitation, including an incentive or time guarantee, to "give us another try."

Database.

If you have the ability to track purchases by consumer, sort the information and invite back those guests who haven't been in for a while. On the flip side, find those who have spent the most money and send them a thank-you gift or free meal for their loyalty.

Build a buzz.

Do unique things such as trivia while you wait, every 100th guest is free, random desserts or appetizers on the house, etc. Advertising is expensive. Buzz is free and attracts attention: "You have to go to _____. They do _____."

> There are plenty of great marketing books to provide ideas to attract guests to the restaurant (Call Pencom International at www.pencominternational.com or visit www.pencominternational.com). None is stronger than word-of-mouth. Implementing the ideas in this book will create a magnet, pulling guests in again and again to experience *Service That Sells!*

chapter fourteen

CHAPTER 14

Action Plan

It's nearly time to get on the floor and begin delivering *Service That Sells!* Is the staff ready? Are the managers ready? Review these items, then see what a restaurant experience looks like when the service sizzles and you can step back and say *Now That's* Service That Sells!

chapter fourteen

Service That Sells! Implementation Checklist

Phase I

- Meet with managers to discuss leading the *Service That Sells!* revolution.
- Conduct employee focus group to gather service suggestions and recommendations.
- Select three to four key employees (hosts and servers) and train them to deliver *Service That Sells!*
- Identify gaps and main priorities for the next 30 days (you can list all the gaps, but focus on only three or four main items initially).
- Conduct staff rally:
  - Describe the "perfect visit" for employees so they can visualize it.
  - Have managers role play "service" vs. *Service That Sells!*
  - Review sizzle points with staff members.
  - Train staff on hospitality and how to say things to guests.
  - Cover situational selling with servers and validate them.
  - Instruct hosts on new seating focus and validate them.
  - Have "test employees" discuss how easy it is, the difference it makes and how much more lucrative it is.
  - Have guests discuss how much better the new service is.
  - Focus on the first two "forks" — regular or first-timer? In a hurry or more casual paced?
- Manage the sizzle, conduct daily shift meetings focused on hospitality, provide constant communication and feedback for staff.
- Talk to guests to get their feedback.
- Model the behaviors and constantly talk hospitality.

Now That's Service That Sells!

Phase II

- Review Phase I — any modifications necessary?
- Identify next set of priorities.
- Work on honing in on customizing the experience (value-driven guests, celebrations, families, carryout, etc.).
- Design sales and service contests to reward progress and encourage sales-building.
- Make necessary adjustments.
- Spread the word in the community — it's time for the neighborhood to get "experienced."
- Dominate the competition!

Now That's Service That Sells!

Restaurant managers' jobs are to provide outstanding guest experiences to make the competition suffer. Competitors, meanwhile, can try to copy the concept, menu and service. As they spend time trying to replicate it, move on to the next level. Always stay one step ahead. You're armed with the secret weapons — the passion to deliver *Service That Sells!* and the ability to reward, recognize and constantly develop the team that provides it — something competitors cannot copy.

Oh, they can hope they can take care of guests adequately, but *Service That Sells!* managers and staff *expect* to deliver service excellence to every guest, every visit. Those managers are conductors and employees the orchestra creating a sizzling experience ....

chapter fourteen

The *Sizzle* Experience

Host

As I entered the restaurant, the host stepped out from behind the stand.

Host: "Welcome to Jim's. You look really familiar — have you been here before?"

Me: "No, this is my first visit."

Host: "Will anybody be joining you tonight?"

Me: "No, just by myself."

Host: "We specialize in service and great food! You're going to have an outstanding meal and you're in luck — tonight we're only on a *short* five- to 10-minute wait. Feel free to visit the bar and try one of our legendary martinis. May I get your name?"

Me: "Schier — spelled S-C-H-I-E-R."

Host (writing down SHEER, like it sounds): "We'll let you know as soon as your table is ready."

As I sat at the bar, Mike, the bartender, introduced himself and shook my hand. Soon after I started enjoying an ice-cold beer.

Seater

Host: "Mr. Sheer, your table is now ready." (Wow, she pronounced my name right!)

I approached the host stand. As we walked to the table...

Seater: "I understand you've never been here before. In case you need them, the restrooms are located near the front door. The restaurant has been here for over 15 years and we recently remodeled. My favorite dish is the blackened chicken pasta and our most popular dish is tonight's special, the grilled salmon. It's outstanding."

Before I knew it, we were at the table (a quiet booth) and I sat down as she placed the guest check on the table and offered me a newspaper to read.

The service assistant approached to fill my water glass and informed me his favorite appetizer was the spinach dip. The server picked up the guest check as she approached.

Server

Server: "Since it's your first time here, may I make a few suggestions?" (How'd she know that?)

Me: "Sounds great."

Server: "I see your beer is pretty full, so I'll ensure there's an ice-cold one waiting for you when you're ready. I'd strongly recommend one of our fish specials there on the insert. We have the best grilled salmon around and my favorite is the blackened tuna."

Me: "I'll try the tuna blackened — medium rare."

Server: "Did you know you can add a Caesar or house salad with our signature dressing for only $1.29? Which would you prefer?"

Me: "I'll try the house'

Server: 'I'll be right back with your salad."

After a great salad, the entrée showed up.

Server: "Here's your blackened tuna. Would you like to take a bite to ensure it's prepared to your liking? (It was.) Enjoy it and I'll be back shortly to check on you."

Manager

A minute or so later...

Server: "Is the tuna as great as I promised?"

Me: "You bet!"

As I was finishing up my tuna, the manager stopped by.

Manager: "Thanks for visiting us tonight. My name is Jim, and you are? I understand it's your first time here. How's the food and service?"

Me: "TJ, and it has been outstanding."

Manager: "Glad to hear that. How did you hear about us?"

Me: "I'm in town for a few days for a conference and some friends told me about it."

Manager: "If you'd like to come back tomorrow, we're featuring mahi mahi. Here's a coupon for a free appetizer if you can make it."

Me: "Thanks!"

chapter fourteen

The server approached.

Server: "We're featuring our signature chocolate mousse cake and an outstanding raspberry cheesecake. If you don't have room for dessert now, you can get it to-go if you'd like. Which would you prefer?"

How can you say "no" to that suggestion?

As I got ready to leave ... Server: "Thanks again for letting us take care of you tonight. I'd be happy to take care of you next time as well."

Now That's **Service That Sells!**

155

appendix a

Appendix

APPENDIX A

Here's a timeline of a guest visit to role play with staff to show how steps of service, if done improperly, don't build business. Set up an area in the dining room with a host stand (or prop) and a table for the role-playing guests to sit at and eat. If there's not enough time, simply role play the critical items for the meeting.

What you'll need:

- Six participants — two to play guests, one server, one host, one service assistant and one manager.
- Plates and glasses to be used for food and drink delivery (don't have to use real food).
- Time to practice various scenes so they can be effectively demonstrated.

Remember, this is how *not* to do it! Over-exaggerate the looks, tone and facial expression so staff will understand how insincere and processed this type of experience is.

Scene I

Guests enter as host writes notes at the stand and doesn't look up.

Guest #1: (Clears throat.)

Host: "Can I help you?"

Guest #2: "We're here to eat dinner."

Host: "We're on a wait."

Guest #1: "But what about those tables over there (pointing)?"

Host: "That section is closed. Name?"

Guest #2: "Smith."

Host: "Wait in the bar, we'll page you when the table is ready."

Host pages party: "Smith, your table is ready." (Guests arrive.)

Host continued: "Two? Follow me (walks ahead of the guests, puts menus down on the table, walks away without ever having said a word)."

appendix a

Buser Greeting

Buser comes up and fills water glasses without saying a word.

Server Initial Greeting

Guests seated at the table. Obviously, they've been there awhile.

Guest #1: "This is taking a while."

Server: "Sorry, I'm swamped. What do you want for dinner?"

Guest #2: "What's good?"

Server: "Everything."

Guest #1: "We'll order drinks. I'll have a draft beer. What kind do you have?"

Server: "I'll have to check."

Guest #1: "Just give me an iced tea."

Guest #2: "I'll have a Coke."

Drink Delivery and Order Taking

Server returns with drinks.

Server: "Who had the iced tea?"

Guest #1: "Me."

Server: "Decided yet?"

Guest #1: "I'll have the special."

Server: "I think we're out. Anything else?"

Food Delivery

Server: "Who had the grilled chicken? Steak?"

Buser

Enters and refills water without saying anything.

Checkback

Server: "Your food still taste OK?"

Guest #1: "Yeah, it's OK."

Manager wanders through the restaurant, not noticing that one of the guests has barely touched the food. Also ignored is the table full of dirty plates, glasses and napkins.

©2010 pencom international · www.pencominternational.com

Dessert Suggestion

>Server: "You don't want dessert do you?"

>Guest #2: "I guess not."

Check Payment

>Server returns with check_____as first guest puts money on the table.

>Server: "You don't need any change do you?"

>Guest #1: "No, that's OK."

Final Busing

>Buser arrives with tub and starts clearing prior to guests getting up to depart.

>Guest #2: "I guess it's time to go."

>Guests get up and walk by host.

Depart at Host Stand

>Host: "Don't forget to tell everyone about the place."

>Guests (in unison): "Don't worry, we will!"

appendix a

Scene 11 — Now *That's* Service That Sells!

Guests enter as host writes notes at the stand. The greeting is immediate.

Host: "Welcome to _____! Today's your lucky day, as we're only on a short five-minute wait. If you'd like to enjoy a drink in the bar, I'll be happy to page you when your table is ready. May I have your name?"

Guest #1: "Smith."

Host: "We'll call you soon!"

Host continued: "Smith party, your table is now available, Smith. (Pause as guests arrive.) Susie, please show the Smith party to their table."

Floor host: "Please follow me, Mr. Smith. Is it your first time here?"

Guest #1: "Sure is."

Floor host: "Great! Thanks for joining us. We are famous for _____, as well as our _____.

In case you're wondering, the restrooms are near the front door."

Once at the table, the guests sit and host opens a menu, pointing to the special.

Floor host: "Our special today is the _____ and Sally, your server, will be right with you. Enjoy your meal!"

Service assistant arrives as you see the host and server talking about the guests being first timers (Host signals #1).

Service assistant: (filling water glasses) "Good evening, gentlemen. My name is _____. Sally and I will be taking care of you tonight. Don't forget to try my favorite appetizer, the _____. It's outstanding! Feel free to let me know if you need anything."

Server: "Mr. Smith, I understand it's your first time here. Thanks for giving us the opportunity to serve you. While you're deciding on your meal, may I offer you a drink?"

Guest #1: "I'll try one of your margaritas."

Server: "Excellent choice — we're famous for those!"

Now That's SERVICE THAT SELLS!

Guest #2: "I'll have a Bud Light and I'd like to try an order of the _____."

Server: "I'll be right back with your drinks and _____. In the meantime, I highly recommend the special today, the _____ or my favorite, the _____."

Server returns with drinks and appetizer.

Server: "Since it's your first time here, may I make a few suggestions or are you ready to order?"

Guest #1: "I'll have the _____."

Server: "Outstanding choice — we get lots of compliments on it."

Server: "And you, sir?"

Guest #2: "I'll have the _____."

Server: "Excellent choice!"

Manager walks by.

Manager: "My name is _____ and I'd like to thank you for dining with us tonight. If your experience is not outstanding, be sure to let me know."

Guest: "Thanks!"

Server: "Looks like you enjoyed your _____! Here's the _____ and _____. Would you please cut into your steak to see if it's cooked to your liking?"

Guest #2: "Sure is!"

Server: "Looks like you enjoyed the margarita! Can I get you another?"

Guest #1: "Certainly."

Server: "I just put another Bud Light on ice for you. Just let me know when you're ready. Enjoy and I'll check back on you shortly."

Server returns with drinks.

Server: "Isn't the _____ outstanding?"

Guest #1: "It's great!"

appendix a

Server: "And your meal, sir, as good as I promised?"

Guest #2: "You bet."

Server: "We're famous for our outstanding desserts including the _____ and the _____ and you can always take them to-go if you're full."

Guest #1: "Let's split a Mud Pie to-go, I'm kind of full."

Server: "Mud Pie to-go, with two forks coming right up!"

Manager arrives.

Manager: "_____ still taking great care of you?"

Service assistant removes plates as server delivers dessert and drops check.

Service assistant: "Does anyone need a refill on their drink?"

Server: "Our famous Mud Pie and two forks ready for the road! Here's your check and I'll take care of that whenever you're ready."

Guests get up to depart.

Server: "Thanks again for dining with us. Hope to serve you again on your next visit!"

Guests: "Thanks!"

Guests walk by host.

Host: "Have a great evening, gentlemen! Thanks for coming in and I look forward to seeing you back here soon!"

Guests: "Certainly!"

APPENDIX B

Now That's Service That Sells!

(For a free downloadable file of this handout,
visit www.pencominternational.com)

Staff Training Handout

Say it differently.

Hosts

Party of two?
___

Four for dinner?
___

Follow me.
___

Thanks.
___

We're on a wait.
___

Name?
___

Smoking or non?
___

appendix b

Server

Hi, I'll be your server today.
_____

Any questions about the menu?
_____

Have you decided yet?
_____

Would you like dessert?
_____

Do you want premium vodka in your drink?
_____

How is everything?
_____

Is everything OK?
_____

Here's your check.
_____

APPENDIX C

(For a free downloadable file of this handout,
visit www.pencominternational.com)

Sizzle Points Handout

HOST: _____
_____
_____
_____

SERVER: _____
_____
_____
_____
_____
_____
_____

SERVICE ASSISTANT: _____
_____
_____
_____

FACILITY_____
_____
_____
_____

PRODUCT_____
_____
_____
_____

photocopying is prohibited

APPENDIX D

(For a free downloadable file of this handout,
visit www.pencominternational.com)

The Pulse Check Card

1) Open the door and welcome arriving guests/thank departing guests.
   - Micro-trash check (out to first row of cars).
   - Glass and brass clean?
   - Floors clean and dry?
   - Great first impression for arriving guests?

2) Welcome a party at the host stand.
   - How long is the wait?
   - Hosts properly welcoming all guests?
   - Menus to waiting guests (activities for kids)?
   - Host stand stocked with all supplies (clean menus, kid's menus, crayons, pens, pagers)?
   - Recognize a host for something outstanding.

3) Seat a party.
   - Listen to other hosts describing specials, identifying why guests are visiting.
   - Any needs at tables you walk by as you seat?
   - Was the guest quoted an accurate wait time?
   - Why is the guest visiting today?
   - Tables need to be cleared? Drink refills? Table maintenance?

4) Make a drink at the bar.
   - Bartender keeping up?
   - Servers suggesting drink specials, wines or premium liquors (look at tickets)?
   - Bar NCO (neat, clean, organized)?
   - All supplies stocked? Change needed?
   - Liquor run needed for back stock?
   - Recognize the bartender for a job well done.

5) Check the restrooms (and send someone of the opposite sex to the other one).
   - Floors clean, debris-free and dry?
   - Mirrors and sinks clean and dry?
   - Toilet paper/paper towels stocked?
   - Restroom checks being done by staff?
   - Check all stalls and/or urinals.
   - Wash hands.

©2010 pencom international · www.pencominternational.com

The Pulse Check Card *(continued)*

6) Deliver food to a table (look around at other tables!).
   - Cook times to standard?
   - Plate presentation top-notch?
   - Listen to other servers as you deliver food.
   - Refills needed, tables clean, checks tendered quickly?
   - Servers having fun and interacting with guests?

7) Check on a guest.
   - Food outstanding?
   - Why are they visiting?
   - Get their names (My name is ____, and you are?).
   - Invite them back.
   - Deliver a free dessert sample or appetizer sample to an unsuspecting guest.
   - Recognize a server and pass on compliments.

8) Make a dish in the kitchen.
   - Cook times to standard?
   - Prep levels maintained?
   - Quality and plate presentation top-notch?
   - Stations clean and organized, sanitation standards met?
   - Take a food temperature (rotate products or areas each hour).
   - Recognize a kitchen team member for something great you just saw.

9) Prepare a carryout order.
   - Phone — selling or taking an order?
   - Order times quoted accurately?
   - Listen to phone — proper greeting, suggestive selling, repeating, thanking?
   - Double-check order — accuracy.
   - Thank staff for being productive, fun and upbeat.

10) Run sales and product mix reports.
    - Sales meeting projection?
    - Product mix – modify any prep items as needed.
    - Communicate with the team — sales needs, running low on items, suggest a specific item, thank them for exceeding goals.
    - Make necessary labor adjustments.

11) Recognize an employee – one per hour (minimum).
    - 30-second review: What is working? What is making their job difficult? How can I help?
    - Praise something done right.

APPENDIX E

(For a free downloadable file of this handout,
visit www.pencominternational.com)

Word Association

Here are a few things commonly thought of when hearing the featured words. Ask employees if any of these were on their list.

Run

Jog, exercise, fast, slow, sweat, work-out, walk (or anything to do with exercise), copies, for office, shift/food/restaurant, election, panty-hose, stockings, on a bank, DMC, Forrest Run, river/creek/water, food, a shift, a restaurant

Sell/Cell

Buy, price, deal, phone, amoeba, biology, division, auction, online, trade-in, financing, deal, battery

Sale/Sail

Price, cheap, deal, garage, boat, wind, mast, catamaran, away

Buy/By/Bi-

Purchase, price, trade, book/author, two (i.e. bicycle), one get one free, sexual

Strike

Bowling, 10 pins, X, stop work, union, ball, baseball, three and you're out, fired, match, punch, hit, blow, lucky (cigarette brand), picket

Fall

> Trip, cool weather, tree, hurt, September, October, November, tumble, take the blame, leaves,

Set

> Dry, cement, glue, harden, tennis/game/match, inflexible, won't change, group of items, taken care of (all set), volleyball

Fair/Fare

> Toll, cost to ride, taxi, bus, rides, amusement, games, equal, proportionate, treatment, OK, medical condition, weather

NOTES

NOTES

NOTES

NOTES

NOTES

NOTES

NOTES

NOTES

GET REAL-WORLD SOLUTIONS WITH SERVICE THAT SELLS!

www.pencominternational.com

Our *Service That Sells!* training products will provide solutions to your toughest management challenges. Pencom International offers a comprehensive line of reality-based management books, training DVDs, and employee workbooks that will help you:

- Improve service
- Increase sales
- Reduce turnover and improve morale
- Increase return guest visits
- Market your operation successfully
- Turn your servers into salespeople
- Transform managers into leaders

Real-World Application

We've been leaders in hospitality training for more than 20 years because products from Pencom International are designed by restaurant operators and managers like you – our real-world experience translates to real-world success for you!

Visit www.pencominternational.com to browse our complete online catalog, read excerpts from our books, view video clips from our *Service That Sells!* and Real World Selling video series, and more, or call 1-800-247-8514 for more information.

Custom Books Also Available!

Wish you could get *Service That Sells!* products customized for your operation? We're here to please! Our books can be easily produced featuring your menu items, your brands, your unique terminology and a custom cover. Visit www.pencominternational.com and click on the "Customized Products" tab for more information.